1/18

D0204919

# WRESTLING WITH LIFE

FOOTPRINTS SERIES

*Jane Errington*, Editor

The life stories of individual women and men who were participants in interesting events help nuance larger historical narratives, at times reinforcing those narratives, at other times contradicting them. The Footprints series introduces extraordinary Canadians, past and present, who have led fascinating and important lives at home and throughout the world.

The series includes primarily original manuscripts but may consider the English-language translation of works that have already appeared in another language. The editor of the series welcomes inquiries from authors. If you are in the process of completing a manuscript that you think might fit into the series, please contact her, care of McGill-Queen's University Press, 1010 Sherbrooke Street West, Suite 1720, Montreal, QC, H3A 2R7.

# Wrestling with Life

## From Hungary to Auschwitz to Montreal

GEORGE REINITZ

with Richard King

McGill-Queen's University Press
Montreal & Kingston · London · Chicago

© McGill-Queen's University Press 2017
ISBN 978-0-7735-5137-4 (cloth)
ISBN 978-0-7735-5183-1 (ePDF)
ISBN 978-0-7735-5184-8 (ePUB)

Legal deposit third quarter 2017
Bibliothèque nationale du Québec

Printed in Canada on acid-free paper that is 100% ancient
forest free (100% post-consumer recycled), processed
chlorine free.

McGill-Queen's University Press acknowledges the support of the Canada Council for the Arts for our publishing program. We also acknowledge the financial support
of the Government of Canada through the Canada Book
Fund for our publishing activities.

**Library and Archives Canada Cataloguing in Publication**

Reinitz, George, 1932–, author
    Wrestling with life : from Hungary to Auschwitz to
Montreal / George Reinitz with Richard King.

(Footprints series ; 25)
Issued in print and electronic formats.
ISBN 978-0-7735-5137-4 (cloth). – ISBN 978-0-7735-5183-1 (PDF). –
ISBN 978-0-7735-5184-8 (ePUB)

    1. Reinitz, George, 1932–. 2. Jews – Hungary – Biography.
3. Holocaust, Jewish (1939–1945) – Hungary – Personal narratives.
4. Holocaust survivors – Québec (Province) – Montréal – Biography.
5. Businesspeople – Québec (Province) – Montréal – Biography.
6. Wrestlers – Québec (Province) – Montréal – Biography.
7. Philanthropists – Québec (Province) – Montréal – Biography.
8. Autobiographies. I. King, Richard, 1945–, author II. Title.
III. Series: Footprints series ; 25

DS135.H93R45 2017       940.53'18092       C2017-902420-5
                                           C2017-902421-3

This book was typeset by True to Type in 11/13.5 Sabon.

# Contents

1934. IX/24.
Marta gyuri

ELIT
/zolnok Gr /zapa

George, age two, with his mother, Marta. The photo was taken by Marta's uncle, Ignac Komaromi, a professional photographer whose specialty was taking photographs of the Hungarian aristocracy.

George, age five, holding a broom behind his back. The idea of holding the broom came from the photographer.

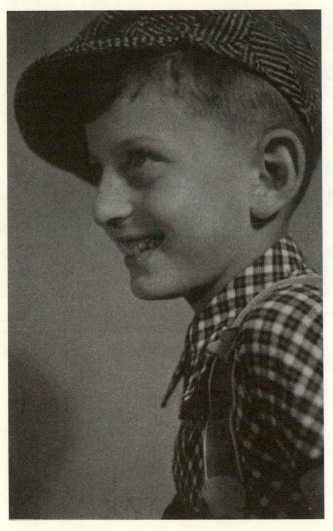

George, age seven. It was around this time that George witnessed his father fighting with the Flums in the synagogue.

George, age ten, with his mother and his sister, Marika, in the dining room of their home in Szikszó. The photograph was taken by his uncle, Dennis Komaromi.

George, age eleven, and his sister Marika, age eight. This photograph was taken in 1943 and is the last photograph of George and his sister before the Holocaust.

George's mother, Marta Reinitz. Photograph by Marta's uncle, Ignac Komaromi.

George's parents, Jacob and Marta Reinitz, in 1940.

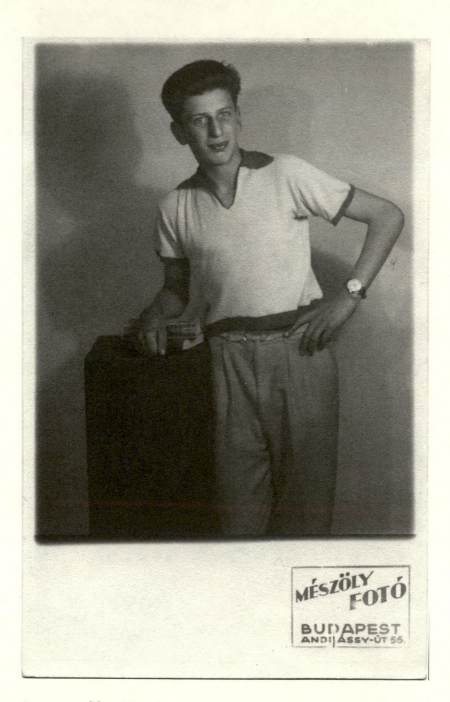

George, age fifteen, just prior to leaving Hungary for Canada. The photo was taken by a professional photographer in Budapest.

George, age fifteen. This was his passport photo, taken in preparation for immigration to Canada.

Dr Alex Grunwald, the man responsible for saving the lives of George and others in the infirmary at Auschwitz. The photo was given to George by Dr Grunwald's widow, Maria Grunwaldova.

American Joint Distribution Committee
Personal History of Child

CHILD  *Reinitz*  *George*

Family name    First name    Any other name    Photograph date taken

*male*    *16 IV 1932*    *Hungary*    *Hungarian*
Sex    Birthdate Day Month Year    Country of birth    Nationality

*Hermina ut 49 Budapest*
Present address of child

Child at present living/underline one/ Children's home-With relatives

Foster family home-Alone

Supported by:

*XIV Hermina ut 49*
Last address of child in country prior to displacement

Description of child:
Color of    Eyes *grey*    Complexion    Hair *brown*
Height/underline one/ Tall    Medium    Short
Weight/    "    " Overweight    Medium    Underweight
Distinguishing marks or features

Personality - Describe how child gets along in school,employment,
with friends,relations or agency workers.What does
he look forward to in new country?

*At school he was ~~only~~ poor student, he was*
*deported when he was 12 years old. At the pre-*
*sent he is apprentice as a metalturner. He*
*does not know yet whether he wishes to continue*
*his trade overseas. He likes reading, has many friends.*
*He is fond of sports, especially football*

In view of above what placement and further education and training
do you recommend?

Education
Present school placement    Last grade completed
Class work/underline one/    good    average    poor *4 grammar*
Occupational training    How long?
Occupational interest
Present employment    *apprentice*    How long?
Languages Read *Hungarian German*
Speak *"    "*
Write *"    "*
Special interests i.e. arts & crafts,music,sports
Orthodox    Non-orthodox

Orphans Project immigration paper. Whoever completed this form recognized George's ability to make friends and his love of sport.

# WRESTLING WITH LIFE

# Introduction

It was my two eldest grandchildren, Amara and Brett, who came up with the idea of this book. They were twenty-one and eighteen at the time and they wanted to know as much as possible about the history of the Reinitz family. They knew about the Holocaust and how it affected me and my family, as I had made every effort to ensure that my children and grandchildren were aware of the history of that dark period generally and how it touched me specifically. But now Amara and Brett wanted to see the town where I was born and spent the early years of my life, and they also wanted to visit Auschwitz to pay their respects to their great-grandparents and all the others who had perished there.

My first reaction to their request was that there were more than enough books on the Holocaust written by better writers than me. I told them I didn't see myself as a writer but I would be more than pleased to answer any questions they had. But I did agree to take them on a trip to Hungary and Auschwitz with their grandmother and me. Our trip to Szikszó, Budapest, Auschwitz, Prague, and Vienna was moving and instructive, and at times, for me, difficult.

If I thought the trip would answer all their questions I was sadly mistaken. Having had the opportunity to visit and see with their own eyes the places that were such an important part of my past and thus of their family history, they had more questions, and their casual request that I write a book about my experiences became a more insistent demand. They wanted to know the details of my life – how, with only a grade six education and after spending time in Auschwitz, I had been able to come to Canada, a new country where I knew no one and didn't speak the language, and make a successful new life for myself. They wanted a written history rather than an oral one so that they would be able to show it to their children and their children's children, and so on into the future. Like grandfathers everywhere, I found it very difficult to say "no" to my grandchildren and so I made up my mind to write the book they requested.

I have to admit that the notion of writing a book recounting my family's history and my own had always been lodged somewhere in the back of my mind, but until I started to work on it I had never fully realized how much effort and talent it takes to write a book. I developed a great deal of respect for writers, and now when I read a book I do so with a greater understanding of what went into its creation. There were times during the process of writing when I felt that I would rather go back to building furniture or to the wrestling that I loved – two endeavours in which I had felt confident.

Remembering the past in order to put it into written form is very different from simply telling those around me about my past. When I told a story, no matter how painful, there was an end to the telling and the conversation moved on to other topics. Writing is permanent. I had to think, and think hard, about those events, many of them very upsetting. This process would keep me up at night. While I slept, my memories found their way into my dreams, and I found myself talking in my sleep. This caused my wife to wake up on many occasions and, although I never told her what I was dreaming about, she knew that the memories I was recording in this book were causing my sleeplessness.

This book tells not only my own story but also stories of the people I met who helped me when I needed it most. Tragically, I lost my parents during the *Shoah* but I was fortunate to have more than one person stand in as a parental figure for me. Because people were so ready to help me when I needed it, I made it my business to lend a helping hand whenever a situation demanded it. I did my best, and continue to do my best, to make every effort to pay back the support I received by paying it forward. I hope that this is one of the messages readers will take away from this book.

I arrived in Canada at the age of sixteen with no immediate family and with nothing in my pockets but my hands. I spoke neither English nor French, and since my education was interrupted by the Holocaust, I never got past the sixth grade level. I knew that if I were to have any success in my new country I would have to work hard for it. I take great pleasure and great pride in the fact that I was able to build a successful business, and I take much greater pleasure and much greater pride in the fact that Eleanor and I now have a family numbering eighteen people and growing. Better yet, all eighteen members of my family are happy, healthy, and hardworking.

Finally, I could not have written this book without help. First and foremost I want to thank Eleanor, my wife, for her support and encouragement in this, and in fact all my endeavours. She is the perfect life partner and I love her all the more for everything she has done to support me. My grandchildren Amara and Brett motivated me to start this project in the first place. I am pleased also to be able to thank my son-in-law Perry Birman (Amara's and Brett's father) for his encouragement and support. My good friend Pina Vellone provided invaluable advice on every aspect of the book. And finally, I want to thank Richard King, who worked with me to make it happen.

# 1

# Szikszó

I came into the world at the worst possible time for a Jewish child to be born in Europe. Ironically, in the dynamic world of North America, for someone who had the attributes necessary to make a success of himself, it was the best possible time to be alive. My life straddled these contradictory historical realities.

I was born on 16 April 1932 in the town of Szikszó (pronounced "sick-so"). Szikszó was then the administrative centre of its district of the province of Abauj. The town itself, with its population of roughly five thousand souls, was located in the northeast corner of Hungary about sixty-five kilometres to the south and west of the border between Hungary and what is now Slovakia but in 1932 was the country of Czechoslovakia. Of this population approximately nine hundred were Jews – fewer than a hundred of whom survived the Holocaust. The rest of the population were Christians, with a smattering of Roma.

A creek called the Manta ran through the town but it was muddy and not suitable for swimming. One of the nice features of our town was that the Hernad River ran near it. In the summer we went to the river by horse and buggy, as it was a pleasant place for families to picnic, swim, and generally enjoy a nice outing.

Szikszó was about seventeen kilometres east of Miskolc, the largest city in the region, which had a population of over 160,000 people before the war. Miskolc was a thirty-minute train ride from Szikszó, and many people from our town commuted to work there or to attend the college in that city, as there wasn't one in our town. Due to its location in a valley in the agrarian area of Hungary, the economy of Szikszó was closely tied to agriculture. This included the rendering of dead animals, which sometimes gave the town a terrible smell.

Szikszó was also a market town, with small markets each week and a huge market twice a year. Vendors would come to the town from all over the province, usually on foot, or by horse and carriage. They had to pay a fee to participate in the market and I remember that there were three major roads to get to the market. Before the farmers and merchants could gain access to the market itself, they were stopped to buy one of the tickets they needed to get into it. The farmers who came to town usually brought animals or products to sell in order to get the money they needed to buy the products they couldn't make or grow for themselves.

The largest hospital in the province of Abauj was in Szikszó, and it was there that I came into the world. I was my parents' first-born and, according to family lore, they were thrilled to have a son. One of my older cousins told me that my father brought me to the second-floor window of the hospital to show me off proudly to his friends. From the day of my birth until the last time I saw my father as he was being marched out of Auschwitz, he never failed to encourage me to do my best and to protect me no matter how dire the situation.

I was told that I developed a serious medical problem within days of my birth. So serious was the malady that my extended family believed there was only a very small chance that I would survive. My father was not a terribly religious man; but neither was he the kind of person not to take advantage of anything that might prove helpful. He went to the rabbi of the town and asked him to say the *Mi Shebierach* (the traditional prayer for the sick) during a Torah reading with my father. I fortunately overcame my medical problem, but I'll never know whether it was the *Mi Shebierach* or the Reinitz fighting spirit that helped me to survive.

\* \* \*

The Szikszó of my childhood was somewhat more modern than the small agricultural villages that surrounded it. After all, the town had electricity and its main thoroughfares were paved with cobblestones. The streets of the outlying villages, even if they had better surfaces than the country roads that linked them, were all unpaved roads. Szikszó, too, had its share of unpaved roads, which became impassably muddy after a thaw or when it rained.

The more prosperous families of the town had telephones, which were both a luxury and a rarity at that time. My family was one of the few that had a phone. Our number had only two digits, the numbers forty-five.

Each of the satellite villages usually had a combination store/ tavern/gathering place where the men could exchange gossip and purchase the necessities for their homes and farms. These places were usually owned by the single Jewish family of the village. Szikszó, by contrast, was home to approximately two hundred Jewish families, and they dominated the business life of the town. The most important of these families was my family – the Reinitz family – which, with all its relations, comprised about fifty people.

My parents lived in Szikszó when I was born but they were not from the town. My father came from the village of Hegymeg, which was twenty kilometres northwest of Szikszó and had a population of less than four hundred people. The town was so small that it didn't have a city hall and didn't keep an official register of births and deaths. This information was kept in the neighbouring town of Lak, about a kilometre and a half away. My father's family of six – his parents, his brother and two sisters, and himself – was the only Jewish family in that village. His father, my grandfather, owned the tavern/general store of that village, which also, when necessary, served as a hotel or inn for the odd traveller who found himself stranded there for a night. My grandfather's general store sold products such as kerosene, salt, sugar, and other things that the peasantry of the region couldn't supply for themselves.

Grandfather also owned a farm that produced various foods, along with milk from his cows. And he owned a vineyard from which he made wine to sell to his customers in the tavern/general store. One of my fondest memories of my grandfather is helping crush the grapes to make wine. All the grandchildren loved to help. Our parents brought us to the vineyard, where we washed our feet and put on a pair of white socks. We were then hoisted into the vats where the harvest of grapes was stored, and we jumped up and down to crush them into the juice my grandfather would then ferment into wine.

At some point before I was born my father's generation of Rein-itzes had moved from the villages to the town of Szikszó. Like his relatives, my father, Jacob, was in business. His first foray into the world of commerce was as a trucker. He owned and drove a truck that made deliveries throughout the region as far away as Szolnok, a city in central Hungary about 160 kilometres from Szikszó.

The Jewish families of Szikszó were to some extent isolated from the larger Hungarian Jewish population, which according to the 1910 census numbered over 900,000 people.* Most of Hungarian Jewry lived in Budapest, which was approximately two hundred kilometres from Szikszó. There was a tendency for Jews who lived in the smaller towns to marry among members of their extended families. My father observed that, as a result of inbreeding among the Jews of the town certain negative physical characteristics, mainly orthopaedic problems, tended to be common in the Jewish community. For example, one of my aunts married a distant cousin and two of their four children suffered from orthopaedic problems. My father had no formal scientific education, so it is a testament to his innate intelligence and his ability to gain insights from his observations that he understood the problems inherent in inbreeding while the rest of the Jews of Szikszó did not appear to understand the relationship between birth defects and inbreeding. Or perhaps they understood the problems but felt powerless to overcome them.

In order to ensure that his children be healthy and free of genetic disabilities, no matter how slight, Jacob chose to marry a woman from the city of Szolnok. Being in the trucking business, he was able to meet people from a larger area than his relatives who lived more circumscribed lives. I don't know exactly how my father met my mother, Marta, but the meeting was more than likely arranged by a matchmaker, a *shadchan*, because that was how things were done in those days. It was the only way a proper and serious Jewish man could meet a Jewish woman of good reputation.

* This information comes from a long article in Wikipedia. https://en.wikipedia.org/wiki/History_of_the_Jews_in_Hungary

My mother's family were more sophisticated and more cultured, and because they were from Szolnok, a good deal less rural than that of my father. My maternal grandfather, Joseph Komaromi, owned a music store and his children were accomplished musicians. My mother played classical music beautifully on the piano. Her brother was a violinist. The youngest in the family, Dennis, her half-brother, played many instruments. He was the rebel of the family and switched from classical music to jazz. When his father, my grandfather, discovered this, he threw Dennis out of the house. Grandfather felt that jazz was an insult to good music and demeaning to the Komaromi family. Dennis came to live with us in Szikszó and remained in our house until he was drafted into the Munkaszolgálatos Brigade, which was a part of the Hungarian army made up of Jews. This brigade had no military role and its sole function was to serve the regular army.

My parents made a handsome couple. My mother was a beautiful woman with fair hair and light skin. She had blue eyes that were soft and loving. Her demeanour was that of a sensitive artist. The casual observer could not have known that she was an accomplished musician but it was obvious that she had the soul of an artist. But first and foremost she was a mother and that meant that she was devoted to nurturing and protecting her children.

My father was a tall man, well over six feet with broad shoulders and an imperious and domineering bearing. No one would call him handsome but he did make a strong impression on all those who met him. His face was dominated by what I call the Reinitz nose – a nose that gives the face character and nobility. My father's authoritative appearance belied an inner softness. He was always ready to help anyone in need and to make certain that everyone who had dealings with him came away happy, feeling better for having dealt with Jacob Reinitz than with anyone else. Like my mother he was a nurturer, but he expressed it differently; he would allow me to take risks that a parent less confident in their son's abilities was unlikely to allow. He was my mentor and my protector, my role model and my support.

In spite of their different backgrounds, urban for my mother and rural for my father, my parents appeared to get along very well. But it must have taken some effort on my mother's part because I remember overhearing her complaining about her husband to some of her friends. My father was typical of men in those days. He saw himself as the dominant figure in the household. Women were expected to stay in the kitchen and not interfere in business decisions. Yet, he recognized that his wife, because of her greater education and more sophisticated urban background, knew about things such as the arts in general and music in particular, subjects of which my father had very little knowledge. Thanks to her influence, he was able to learn about these things and develop an appreciation for them.

In other ways my father was a very modern, progressive type of person. He hired full-time household help to assist my mother with the cooking and cleaning. His style of dress and his approach to business was not at all common in Szikszó in those days. He dressed in a suit and insisted on having his shoes shined daily. He adopted the style of a cosmopolitan businessman and had business dealings with companies from outside the country.

Three years after I was born my mother gave birth to my sister, Marika. She was a pretty little girl and looked very much like my mother. As children, my sister and I fought a lot, as many siblings do. I had feelings of jealousy toward her as I felt that my father gave her more attention than he gave me. Marika, for her part, did not shy away from this sibling rivalry and she would squeal on me whenever she discovered that I was doing something wrong. When I was a youngster I used to sometimes sneak away for a smoke. It was the kind of thing that made me feel very grown up. My sister would tell on me when she found me smoking a cigarette.

These conflicts with my sister didn't really disrupt my life in any way. I was an active kind of kid; I much preferred to play soccer with my friends than to learn the piano from my mother. My friends and I were typical of all kids in that we liked to do things that were potentially dangerous without much thought to their consequences. In the winter the Manta Creek would freeze over and we would go ice-skating on it. As the creek thawed in the spring we would continue to skate. We were a group of daring kids and we didn't mind taking the risk of falling through the melting ice. As the creek thawed, the ice didn't quite reach the shore so we would have to take a running jump in order to get onto the frozen part of the water and jump back to shore in the same way. Sometimes we landed hard on the ice and went into the freezing waters of the creek. Luckily the river was not deep but we did get thoroughly soaked. When I got back to shore the other kids and I would build a fire so we could dry off and warm up. I was worried that if I went home in wet clothes my father would kill me!

In spite of the growing anti-Semitism in Hungary generally and in Szikszó in particular, I had a happy childhood. I did all the things the other kids in the town did. At that time all the towns and villages had a town crier, a very important figure in our lives. The kids of Szikszó used to follow the town crier as he walked through the town beating his drum. When the townspeople heard the sound of his drum they would come out of their houses, curious about what he would report. When he had gathered a crowd he would take out his notes and read the so-called news. Often he was the only person in town who could read. The news he read was really propaganda. He would report, for instance, that the Germans were occupying towns in the Ukraine and Russia and that the Axis war effort was going well. He would intersperse these stories with local information about some guy's horse going into another guy's barn and other small domestic problems. The idea was, I guess, that the small stories about town life lent credence to the larger stories about the war.

By and large we had a good family life. By the time my father was married with children, he had given up his trucking business and had a business trading in agricultural products, mainly oats, barley, and similar produce. He bought grains from the farmers in the region and sold them to flour mills and beer companies. Because our town was located so close to the border with Czechoslovakia, my father sold much of what he bought to Czech brewers.

We had a very nice house in Szikszó that was modern for its time and place. I remember that my father organized and supervised its construction. Because he was tall, the builder would measure him to be certain that the doors were built to accommodate his height. There was a large bedroom that my parents shared, and a second room – a family room where we spent most of our time. Until I was about eight years old all four of us slept in my parents' room. Then, after I turned eight my sister continued to sleep in my parents' room but my parents moved me to a bed in the family room. During the day my sister and I did our homework in this room and in the evening it was where we gathered as a family to listen to the radio. We also had our family meals in this room. There was a dining room, which was only used on special occasions, and, of course, a kitchen.

Our house was one of the first in the town to have indoor plumbing. We even had the luxury of a bathtub. In those days the plumbing was designed with a well in the basement. We used to pump water up to a tank in the attic that would supply our sinks and bathtubs with a turn of the faucet. A small heater provided us with hot water when we needed it so we didn't have to boil water for washing and for baths. We still had to use the outside toilet sometimes, though.

The house was well furnished and had a very nice garden where fruit and vegetables grew. We were rich enough that money was never a problem. We also had a staff of people to help out with the housework. One of the workers, a young woman named Margit, was with us for many years and we were very close to her. She was one of the few people that I sought out when I visited Szikszó in 1978 with my wife, Eleanor, and our children. Our former maid was the only person who was genuinely happy to see me and my family on that trip. She practically collapsed with joy and couldn't stop herself from crying. We were all very affected by the emotion of the experience.

Father's warehouse and office were on the same property as our house. This was a very convenient arrangement for him in that he could come home for lunch every day. Behind the warehouse was a stable where we had some horses. We also had a couple of cows. My father bought them because they were some kind of extraordinary cows that gave especially rich milk for us. He wanted us to have the best. There were a couple of workers who looked after the stable and the livestock.

We had only two cows, but there was a farmer who had a herd of cows that used to pass by our house on the way to graze. He included our cows in this herd. One day, when the cows returned to the barn, the door was closed. This was odd because our employee who worked with the cows always left it open for them. I saw that there was a problem and I went across the yard to open the doors for the cows. I must have been around seven at the time. When I opened the doors I immediately understood why they had been shut. The guy who looked after the cows had hanged himself behind the door. His tongue was hanging out of his mouth. The police came and interviewed me and I felt very important because I had to sign some official documents. My mother was very worried that this experience would be a shock to me and would scar me psychologically. For some reason that was never explained to me, she made me drink a lot of water. I guess she thought this would help me cope. But, in truth, the experience, sad though it was, didn't shock me at all.

The man who hanged himself was obviously depressed. His pig had apparently died and that meant that his family wouldn't have enough food for the winter. The Hungarian peasantry depended very heavily on the ownership of at least one pig that could be nurtured to the point where it could be slaughtered, thus providing food for a year while a replacement pig was brought to maturity. The loss of a pig meant disaster for the family that owned it. This was what must have pushed the poor man over the edge to make him take his life.

My mother was happiest when she was playing the piano. My sister and I and her music were the things that she lived for. She was a loving and giving person and we loved and admired her in return. She would joke with me that I was like my father in all ways except one – I had her blue eyes. I see those blue eyes every time I look in a mirror and I'm reminded of my mother's love for me and mine for her.

My mother's concern for her children expressed itself in all the normal ways. She nurtured us and worried about us, especially about me as I was a risk taker and my father encouraged this side of my personality. Mother's pragmatic and nurturing nature also expressed itself in small acts of kindness, certain things she did every day. I remember one thing in particular.

Like all other kids in the town my sister and I walked to school – it was about a kilometre from our house. In the winter our mother would give each of us a baked potato to put in our mittens to keep our hands warm. She would put some butter and salt in our school bags so when we got to school we would have a warm snack. I don't think any of the other kids' mothers thought to do this. It was this kind of thing that made my mother special.

Although I didn't share my mother's love of music when I was a child, as I became older and more established in life her cultural influences became apparent. My wife and I attend concerts whenever possible, and operas such as *La Bohème* and *Madame Butterfly* have the power to move me to tears. I'm certain that my love of music is due to my mother's influence and a way of honouring her. Even today, more than seventy years later, I have vivid dreams of my mother playing her favourite pieces on the piano.

\* \* \*

We had a happy family life, but I was not very old before I began to recognize that all was not well in Szikszó and in the rest of Hungary. Indications of the trouble to come started to appear in the town. Signs were posted here and there, anti-Semitic signs that said, "Jews go to Palestine" and "Jews Get Out of Here." As children we felt the sting of anti-Semitism when we were chased in the street by the Gentile children yelling taunts such as "dirty Jews."

In Szikszó, as in most small towns and villages in Eastern Europe, Jews didn't mix with Gentiles. The two communities lived separately, coming into contact only when necessary for trade or other business reasons. Most of the businesses in the town, such as textile and clothing manufacturing and hardware, were owned by Jews. And most of the professionals such as the doctors and lawyers were also Jewish. Gentiles controlled the banks, the administration of the town, and all levels of government.

The townspeople used to spread rumours that when Jews controlled a certain kind of business they took advantage of their position and fixed prices to the detriment of the customers. Two of my relatives were in the hardware business and they suffered because of such stories. Being a child, I had no real idea of what went on in the world of business but I understood that this kind of innuendo caused a certain amount of friction between the two communities. Rumours did not cause the *Shoah* but they did set a tone of hostility and mistrust that made it possible.

We were taught not to like the Catholic community and to
think of the Catholic priest of Szikszó as an enemy, even though I
know that my father had many discussions with the man and
liked him. Our rabbi didn't want us to mix with the Gentiles. The
rabbi was a very orthodox cleric and his solution to the problem
of anti-Semitism, which was obviously growing, was to tell us to
pray more intensely. He believed that the root of the problem was
that we weren't praying with enough devotion and that the anti-
Semitism we had to endure was God's way of telling us we
weren't sufficiently observant. If we prayed harder and more fer-
vently, things would surely get better. He urged us to be *frum*, a
*Yiddish* term meaning to carefully observe all the Jewish religious
laws. But all this did was encourage us to remain passive and igno-
rant. No matter how hard we prayed – and we prayed like crazy –
things got worse and worse.

I may have been a child at the time that the rabbi preached this
way, but even at such a young age I was surprised that we Jews did-
n't get together to show some force, to stand up for ourselves, to
fight back. I felt then, and I feel now, that this would have been
better than praying and relying on God to fight our battles.

Of course we never did anything combative. Within our community we had a close and supportive relationship among ourselves. We were peaceful and believed strongly that God would be
there for us when we needed him as long as we lived good Jewish
lives, which consisted of following the rules of the religion, praying, and helping one another. We did all these things, or at least we
tried to. We went to synagogue every day. And we did our best to
help those in need. For example, there was a *Yeshiva* (a school dedicated to the study of the *Torah*) in our town and some of the students there were from towns other than Szikszó. We made certain
they were cared for and were fed, and members of our community invited them into their homes and treated them as family members. We believed it was important to show concern for those who
needed help, especially those who were devoting their lives to
studying the *Torah*.

The Jews and the Gentiles of Szikszó did not mix socially, but
there was another group of people in our town who were looked
down on by both communities – the Roma. They lived in mud

houses opposite the town, on the other side of the Manta Creek. We referred to this area as Gypsy Town. Jews and Gentiles both unfairly perceived the Roma as a nuisance. They tended to be musicians at one of the bars in our town or would do odd jobs. Jewish people would hire them to cut wood for their fires and other such manual chores. Those who were not involved in either of these endeavours either stole or begged. Most of the families of Szikszó kept dogs as pets but also as a protection against being robbed. Those of the Roma who were thieves developed a method of getting past the canine burglar alarms. They would feed the dogs chunks of bread with needles concealed in them. And as the dogs choked on the needles they could neither bark nor chase the robbers, who now had access to our houses.

*  *  *

My sister and I went to a private Jewish school in Szikszó. This gave us all even less opportunity to mix with and befriend Gentile children. In fact the school system was set up to keep Jewish and Gentile children apart. I don't know if my parents would have allowed me to attend a secular school if Hungary hadn't had those laws.

The day school itself was not religious; it taught the curriculum set by the government. But there was also a religious school, a *cheder*, attached to the school I attended. From the age of six on I attended *cheder* after classes in my regular school. The *cheder* expected me to wear the religious *tzitzit* (the fringes that hang from an undergarment that religious Jews wear) but I rarely did. When I was asked why I was not wearing them, I would say that they were in the washing. The teacher must have thought I had the cleanest *tzitzit* in Szikszó because they were in the washing most of the time.

In our free time we used to play soccer in the schoolyard. It wasn't an organized league or anything; it was just a pick-up game. All the kids who played soccer with me were Jewish with the exception of my best friend, Jeno, who lived next door to me. For some reason the other kids in the neighbourhood thought Jeno was Jewish and they used to chase him, yelling anti-Semitic chants. Poor Jeno never really understood why he was being chased.

I would describe myself as a rough kind of a kid. I loved sports and I never shied away from a fight. I learned from my father not to tolerate any kind of disrespectful or bullying behaviour. When I was growing up I witnessed on more than one occasion a situation where my father showed his disposition to take on anyone he thought behaved badly.

The event that I best remember occurred when I was seven or eight years old at the synagogue we attended. In Szikszó the synagogue was more than a place of religious worship; it was a gathering place where the men of the town could exchange information on town events, Hungarian politics, and the progress of the war. My father and I attended *shul* on a regular basis for both religious and secular reasons. One day while we were at morning prayers, my father noticed that Mr Flum, a member or our congregation, spat on the floor. This was shockingly inappropriate behaviour to say the very least. My father, who prided himself on his neat appearance and the fact that he always behaved with propriety, was horrified by Mr Flum's act of egregious disrespect. It was not in his nature to allow such an act to go unchallenged. He went to where Mr Flum was seated, grabbed him by his jacket collar and told him to get out of the synagogue and go to a stable where he belonged. My father was easily a foot taller than Mr Flum and his anger was not to be taken lightly.

Mr Flum's two adult sons and some of their friends came to his defence and told my father he had no right to accost the man, that he didn't own the synagogue, and that he should mind his own business. My father was not in any way intimidated by Mr Flum's sons and their friends, and was more than prepared to back up his demand with force if necessary. But he was also aware that I was with him and his first impulse was to ensure my safety. He picked me up and placed me on a window ledge high enough to keep me out of the dispute, with the admonition to stay put. He then turned his attention back to the Flums, and a fight broke out. My father's younger brother, Willy, like all Reinitz men tall and broad and strong, joined the fray, and I have a powerful memory of cheering for the Reinitz brothers as they fought the Flums and their friends, ultimately emptying the synagogue. My dad and I attended *shul* many more times together over the years and at no time did anyone have the nerve to behave as badly as Mr Flum did.

In the *cheder* I attended, the students were less controlled than in the regular school, and there were a couple of bullies who picked on the weaker kids. I was the one who protected them. The reason the bullies could get away with their behaviour was that the teacher at the *cheder* mostly slept while we were supposed to be studying. I had the advantage of being taller and stronger than most of the kids in the class and that was why I was ready to stand up to anyone who wanted a fight. I had a close friend in the school by the name of Laci, who was also tall and, like me, a tough kid.

Neither Laci nor I liked *cheder*; we would rather have been outdoors playing sports. The teacher called our fathers to the school and complained that we were not learning anything and that we needed a tutor. So the two fathers hired a *bucher* (a student) from the Yeshiva to tutor us. The tutor came to my house by bicycle. When we took a break from studying so that he could eat a snack my mother prepared for him, I would sneak out and let the air out of his tires. When he went to my friend's house he would do the same thing. So, even though we had a tutor, we didn't really learn anything. When the teacher again complained to my father, my father said, "Why don't you hit him?" I guess he thought that was a way to get me to attend to my lessons. One day the teacher decided to take my father's advice and he came at me with a stick, prepared to hit me. I jumped out of my seat and took the boxer's pose with both fists raised, ready to hit the teacher if he tried to smack me with his stick. Laci also got up and was prepared to fight. When the teacher saw us standing there, ready to defend ourselves, he ran out of the classroom. Now, as then, I don't look for a fight but I don't run away from one if it finds me.

Even as a kid I was curious about different religions and interested in their history. I identified myself as a Jew but didn't believe that prayer would solve our problems. My opinion has not changed much over time. I'm very proud to be Jewish but I still have a great deal of difficulty believing in and following the rules of the religion. When I speak about my experiences during the Holocaust to groups of students I'm often asked if I prayed to God while in Auschwitz. I don't want to disillusion the students, so I avoid answering the question by telling them I'm only in their school to talk about my experiences during the Holocaust, not to get into religious issues.

Although my father went to the synagogue every day, he went as much to meet the other men of the town and to exchange news and gossip as for religious reasons. The synagogue was a meeting place. In fact there were two synagogues in Szikszó and both of them were beautiful buildings. We were a religious family, ortho-dox, but also secular in that we didn't wear *payot* (side curls), my father didn't have a beard, and, as I explained, I avoided wearing the *tzitzit* as much as possible. My mother kept a kosher household and we had two sets of dishes. These were the regular observances of a Jewish family and we didn't go much beyond that.

My family were well off financially and we believed that as long as we prospered and dealt honestly with our suppliers and our cus-tomers we would live through the difficult war years and things would return to normal after the war ended. I suspected then and I know now that we were naive in our beliefs. We had faith in our rabbi and we were always optimistic. In addition, we were badly misled by members of our own community, fellow Jews who con-vinced us that things were not as bad as they actually were.

There was a group of Jewish representatives from Budapest, res-pected leaders of the Jewish community there, who visited our town and others like it. They were sent out to garner support for the Hungarian government in its war against the Russians. These men did their best to convince us that the Soviet Union was a more serious threat to us than the Nazis. They played on our sense of Hungarian nationalism. Yes, we were Jewish, but we were also Hungarian and we believed that our loyalty to the Hungarian state was of extreme importance. So it was easy to convince us that the Russians were the real enemy – communists who sought world domination. We believed them and our community supported the Hungarian government in its fight against Russia, even going so far as to send packages to the soldiers on the Russian front.

These Jews from Budapest came to our synagogue to speak to us, to gain our support for the government, but they had no direct con-nection with our rabbi. They only made contact with him in order to have a place to speak to us – a place that would give the impression that they had our best interests at heart. These men knew that if they spoke to us from the *bimah* of our synagogue it would lend credence to their remarks. As Jews they understood full well the important role the synagogue played in our lives and knew we wouldn't think anyone would lie to us in that hallowed building.

I have a very strong memory of one of these imposing men who came to speak to us at our synagogue. He was an elegant gentleman, very well dressed and very well spoken. I don't think I ever knew what this man did but through his dress and his bearing he gave the impression that he was a lawyer or a banker – in other words an authority figure. The people of Szikszó were not as assimilated as he was. Most of the Jewish men in our town were devoted to their religion. The man who spoke at our synagogue told us not to worry. "I have spoken to the head of the Gestapo," he said. "And yes, anti-Semitism exists but it is not altogether the fault of the Gestapo. It is the newspapers that are making it worse than it really is." He went on to say that he knew the head of the Gestapo and that he was not a bad guy. "I am here to tell you that he is a family man and it is the job of the Jewish community to support the state against the Russians."

The Jewish leaders who spoke to us were liars and hypocrites. Under the leadership of Rudolf Kasztner, they negotiated a deal with the Nazis. They were promised safe passage to Switzerland for themselves and their families if they proselytized to their co-religionists in favour of the Hungarian regime.

Of course I didn't know the full details of the betrayal of Kasztner and his allies at the time; I was only a child. I found out later from a close friend of mine who knew the history of Hungary during the war and the Nazi occupation and who followed the Kasztner trial in Israel. It is true that Kasztner saved the lives of 1,684 Jews but his, and his friends' collaboration with the Nazis sent the mass of Hungarian Jewry to their deaths. He knew the fate of the women and children in the camps because he visited them before the Hungarian deportation.

Kasztner had a moral and ethical obligation to find a way to warn us of the fate that awaited us if we followed the Nazis' orders. Had we known the truth, we might have found a way to defend ourselves. Instead, we were convinced to believe the big lie that, yes, we were being deported, but our families would be kept together and, other than the inconvenience of being resettled, no harm would come to us. Countless Jews went to their deaths because our own leaders were complicit in the Nazi deception.

The situation of my dear friend Paul Herczig is an example of how families were made to accept deportation. In 1944 Paul was a seventeen-year-old apprentice electrician living with his parents in the area around Budapest. There was a great demand for people with his skills to work in the factories that were producing equipment for the war effort. Jews who possessed Paul's skills were exempt from deportation if they worked in one of those factories. But while Paul was with his mother and father at an embarkation point for Jews being sent out of Budapest, an announcement was made that skilled workers could remain behind. So Paul and his parents, believing that nothing horrible awaited them, chose to remain together as a family.

Because the Herczig family believed the lies of the Nazis and their Hungarian quislings, including Kasztner, that they were being sent to some sort of work camp and not to a death camp, they agreed to allow Paul to accompany them when they were deported. If Paul's parents had known the truth they would, without question, have forced Paul to remain in Budapest and take the factory job. It would surely have broken their hearts to be separated from their son but they would have had the satisfaction of knowing they had saved his life.

* * *

Slowly and surely, over the 1930s and 1940s, the government in Budapest passed more and more anti-Semitic legislation. First there were laws restricting the kinds of businesses Jews could own. Then there were laws forbidding Jews from being able to export products. These laws were followed by prohibitions against Jews hiring domestics and laws that forbade religious intermarriage. There were even laws governing the kind of radios Jews could own. Our radios were restricted to one vacuum tube and could only receive government-controlled radio stations. All we could listen to was government propaganda. We were forbidden from having radios that could pick up signals from outside the country. A representative of the government came to Jewish houses to ensure that their radios conformed to the law and then the radios were sealed. In other words, Hungary was a very anti-Semitic country.

Even as life was becoming tougher for the Jews of Hungary, my father believed that we were Hungarians as well as Jews and that we had an obligation to support the state. My grandfather had died in the late 1930s, and by the early 1940s my father had taken over the farm that his father had owned. Father believed that our role in the agricultural life of the country made us essential producers of the food our country needed.

In spite of the anti-Semitic laws, my father continued to believe that if we were established agricultural producers we would be able to ride out the difficult times and would survive. He became friendly with a Mr Faji, one of the big landowners of our area, who had a huge farm in a small town not far from Szikszó. The name of the town was Felsővadász and it was about twenty kilometres north of Szikszó. Mr Faji was in some way connected to one of the aristocratic families of Hungary. He owned thousands of acres of land and had all kinds of animals. His farm was not modern; he was still plowing his fields with horses rather than machinery. Mr Faji's main interest was not agriculture but gambling, and he spent as much time as he could in Monte Carlo. Father spoke with him many times and was able to make a deal with him to rent his farm. Father agreed to pay him enough in rents that Mr Faji could spend as much time and money in Monte Carlo as he wished.

Pigs were very important to the agricultural economy of the region. As I mentioned earlier, it was the loss of his pig that had caused our employee to commit suicide in our barn. Gentile farmers sold pigs in the local market. Obviously, Jewish people did not and could not raise pigs. This became a special problem when my father rented Mr Faji's farm and took over its management. There were about forty pigs that made up part of the livestock on the farm and according to rabbinic law we were not permitted to raise them. My father would not finalize a deal until he had the rabbi's approval.

Whenever a problem of this magnitude occurred it was taken to our rabbi for adjudication. After lengthy discussion between the rabbi and my father, a solution was found. The manager of Mr

Faji's farm, a man by the name of Mr Mata, would be responsible for the management of the pigs. Mr Mata received 10 percent of the profits of the farm, which meant that his share of the profits came from raising and selling the pigs. In this way my father would not be involved with breeding and raising pigs. My father was content with this solution because it satisfied rabbinic law. But he had a second reason for liking the rabbi's solution. Mr Mata lived on the farm and acted as a general manger when father was not there. My father·thought that because he received a share of the profits he would be motivated to be a good manager.

Father had two motives in renting the farm from Mr Faji. The first was that, due to the anti-Semitic laws his business licenses had been revoked and it was now difficult for him to operate his grain-trading business. The second was that father believed that as a farmer he was serving the interests of the country and the economy, and that he was a good citizen providing food for the people and therefore would not be bothered by the government.

We never lived on the farm; we remained in our house in Szikszó. My father would spend at least one day a week at the farm and he would get there by horse and buggy as he didn't own a car. In the winter when we visited the farm, instead of riding in the carriage we would walk behind it so we wouldn't freeze. In addition to running the farm my father still had his grain warehouse, but it was now used for warehousing the products we produced on the farm. I spent as much time as I could with my father, especially in his warehouse. I loved to hang around and learn all I could about his business.

One of my strongest and best memories from my childhood involves the farm. We had horses on the farm and I wanted to ride the wild horses that no one else could ride. So my father made a deal with me: if I got a good report card he would allow me to ride one of the wild horses. In Canada when a kid gets a good report card he gets something material, but all I wanted was to ride a horse that no one else had been able to ride. My mother was not in favour; she worried that I would injure myself. My father told her, "If he wants to kill himself then let him kill himself," and he let me ride the wild horses. I understood perfectly that my father didn't want me to hurt myself, much less kill myself – it was his way of teaching me to take on a challenge and succeed. The experience with the wild horses and my father's support taught me a valuable lesson: that if I believed in myself, I could do anything. This is a lesson that helped me in my life generally, both in my business life and in the sport of wrestling. It especially helped me when I was a prisoner in Auschwitz. As we shall see, my knowledge of horses and my ability to take care of them saved my life.

We modernized the farm. We provided income for the people who worked for us, and we provided food for the Hungarian people. We saw ourselves as loyal citizens of the country. None of this made the slightest difference. The Nazi-controlled Hungarian government took everything we had built and committed itself to the destruction of Hungarian Jewry.

Despite all his efforts to prove himself a loyal Hungarian, Father understood that we were at risk and he made a trip to Budapest to try to get entry visas to Canada, the United States, or England. He was unsuccessful in all three cases. To this day, I am deeply upset – angered is a better way to put it – when people talk about how much Roosevelt or Mackenzie King, or even Churchill, did to support innocent victims during the war against the Nazis, because I have firsthand knowledge of how little they did to save European Jews. They actually refused to help and it is well known that they denied entry to their countries of boatloads of Jewish refugees, thereby delivering them to the Nazis to be murdered. It angers me when I wonder, as I often do, how many Jews would have been saved from the gas chambers if these three leaders had acted in a more humanitarian way.

In 1942 groups of Polish Jews passed through our town. There were a lot of them and they came in whatever transport they could find, mostly cars and trucks. We asked them where they were going and they explained that they were heading to Palestine. They warned us not to stay in Hungary. They warned us of the Nazi atrocities that were being committed in Poland, that people were being tortured, that people were being taken from their houses and lined up and shot. It would only be a matter of time, they told us, before it happened in Hungary and it would be best for us to get out while we could. We didn't believe them. We surmised that they had done something wrong and that they had not been not

loyal to their country. We believed that as loyal Hungarian citizens
we would not have the same problems. Of course we knew about
the anti-Semitic elements in our country and our government and
we fought them as best we could. But, at that time, we didn't turn
our backs on our country. I don't know what we would have done
if we had believed what those refugees told us, but the sad fact is
that we didn't believe them and their predictions came true.

\* \* \*

The Hungarian army fought on the side of the Germans and was
heavily involved in the war on the eastern front. The government
drafted Jews into a special work brigade that was sent to serve the
needs of the army. A lot of Jews were sent far into Russia and Ukraine
to perform manual tasks for the regular army. This included being
sent out into the fields to pick up land mines. Many Jews lost their
legs performing this task. Other tasks that Jews were forced to perform were a little less dangerous, tasks such as carrying food and
ammunition for the army. The Jews were not given uniforms and
had to wear their own clothes. They worked very hard and were treated very badly. Punishments were meted out to these workers on the
slightest pretext whenever they failed to obey one of the many rules
that governed their work.

When my father was drafted into one of these work battalions,
he was not sent to the front, owing to the fact that he had varicose
veins. He was stationed near enough to Szikszó that we could visit
him every weekend. He was away in the labour battalion during
the harvest period when the farmers would bring their crops to
our warehouse while we still had our business in 1942. Mother
took on the responsibility of dealing with the farmers. My father
granted me permission to handle the scales that weighed the crops
the farmers brought in. The weight determined how much we
would pay them. I always manipulated the scales so that the farmers would get a little bit extra. This practice annoyed my mother,
who told me that by doing this I was cheating myself. I argued that
giving a little bit extra would make the farmers feel good. But I
couldn't convince mother of this. She said, "Don't cheat them and
don't cheat yourself." On one of our visits to my father, she com-

plained to him about my practice of giving a little bit more. I was very happy when father gave me the go-ahead to continue this practice. "I'm very proud of you," he told me. And I continued this practice of giving a little bit more throughout my business life.

My sister was too young to have anything to do with my father's business. She was very much like our mother in that she was more interested in practising the piano than playing sports or that kind of thing.

The lessons I learned from my father helped me throughout my life. My father was a strong man in every sense of the word. It was his strength of character that served as my role model in life. As a businessman in the grain trade he had a lot of employees. He did his best to be friendly with them and to help them in any way he could. That was his nature. He operated his business according to a very simple idea: if you treat people well they will provide the extra effort needed to make a business a success. He believed that it was a very bad idea to take advantage of your employees, as this would only give them licence to take advantage of you. When he noticed that his employees were working too hard he encouraged them to take a break so as not to risk their health by overdoing it. This gave his workers the sense that they were valued. I applied this principle that I learned from my father to the businesses I owned and operated.

I mentioned earlier that Jews were not permitted to own radios that picked up a signal from outside Hungary. However, one of our neighbours' kids got some wiring and figured out how to make a radio that could pick up the BBC. Mother was able to understand some English, so we got some idea of what was taking place in the rest of Europe. By 1943 we learned that the Germans were facing defeat at Stalingrad and we had hopes that the Germans and their Hungarian allies, who were also fighting on the eastern front, would start to lose the war and that the Russians would start pushing them back. We also knew that the Americans and the British were planning to land in Europe and we were hopeful about this as well. But we hoped in vain.

Following the end of the First World War, Hungarian politics had been chaotic. The government in power up to mid-October 1944 was led by Miklós Horthy. He was allied with the Axis powers but he tried to steer a somewhat independent course. He passed the anti-Semitic legislation demanded by his German masters but he did his best to retard the deportation of Hungary's Jews. He succeeded in this until the Germans invaded Hungary in March 1944, and from that point forward he was no longer able to protect the Jewish population of Hungary.

I was in school, in the fifth grade, when the teacher came in and told us that the Germans had occupied our country. This was on 19 March 1944. Even though Horthy remained in office until October 1944 when he was replaced by the murderous fascist Ferenc Szálasi, leader of the Hungarian Arrow Cross Party, the Germans, under the direction of Adolf Eichmann, were already calling the shots. For the Jews of Hungary this was the beginning of the end.

It took the Germans barely one month following the occupation of Hungary to start the deportations to the death camps. We soon heard that the authorities were rounding up the Jewish population of our area for deportation. First they took the rabbi, who was the leader of our community. We had also heard from the other towns in the region that they were gathering Jewish people and removing them from their houses. We had no idea where they were being taken.

My family was picked up by the local police on 17 April 1944, one day after my twelfth birthday. They told us they had orders to take us to the city hall and we had one hour to get our belongings together. One hour! How do you pack a family's life into sixty minutes? Even now, all these years later, it is hard to describe the fear and anger that overwhelmed me when I was a twelve-year-old child facing a terrifying and unknown future with my family.

My mother, ever practical, had prepared for our deportation with the same forethought that she used to give us hot potatoes to keep our hands warm as we walked to school in the winter. She prepared some cookies so we would have some food and she baked her jewelry into some of the cookies in case we needed it for bribes. We could also use the jewelry to buy food if that became necessary.

While we were leaving our home with our few belongings we saw people waiting outside who were very happy that we were being taken away. As soon as we left our house we saw those people going into it and ransacking it. We could see the townspeople, our former neighbours, taking our menorahs and other belongings. This hurt.

But the thing that hurt me the most was having to leave my dog behind. I had a dog – his name was Boudri – a mixed breed, part German Shepherd but not quite as big. He was a great friend to me and I was very attached to him. When I came back to Szikszó a couple of years later I found Boudri and I was very disappointed that he didn't recognize me.

I've been back to Szikszó twice since I left it after the war. On both occasions it was not my idea to return to the town. My children and then my grandchildren wanted to see the town I came from so I agreed to visit Szikszo with them. But the Szikszó we visited in no way resembles the town of my childhood.

The houses where my family and friends lived have been neglected and were in a dilapidated state when we saw them on our last visit. Our once-beautiful synagogues have been turned into cultural centres. The people of Szikszó go about their daily lives choosing to forget that the town once had a thriving, productive, and happy Jewish population. They seem to feel that getting rid of the Jews was good for them because now they have the houses that the Jews used to own.

In some ways I can't fully blame the Gentile population of Szikszó. I understand that they were fed a lot of anti-Jewish propaganda by an anti-Semitic government and the Catholic Church, and they believed it. It is even possible that, in the early days of the occupation, they didn't know what would happen to us because we didn't know either. But they know now and their seeming ignorance seems willful.

It does trouble me that when I went back and talked to the people of Szikszó there was no sign that they recognized or regretted what happened to us or acknowledged the catastrophe we endured. They all wanted something *from* me. I was asked to help to build an arena that would be named after me. One couple asked if I would help their daughter by sponsoring her to come to Canada. It is part of my nature and a big part of the lessons I learned from my father and from the many other people who provided me with guidance in life, to extend a helping hand whenever possible;

but in this case I could not bring myself to do that, and I chose not to accede to their requests.

Even the odd person who I found to be modern and congenial, a family that had been friends of my father's, for example, could not or would not discuss the events of the past. Even when I made the comment that we had suffered and they had received all the benefits, I couldn't get them to acknowledge what had happened to us. I understand that they couldn't undo the past, but it would have been nice if the people of Szikszó had at least shown some sympathy for the events of the past. The only person who showed us any respect, who was genuinely happy to see me again and meet my family was, as I have mentioned, Margit, the woman who was our maid when I was a child.

My two visits to Hungary were very difficult for me emotionally. When I was growing up in Hungary they treated me as a "dirty Jew," and when I visited the country I felt that the people still saw me in that way. It took me a while to get over the upset of these visits and to get back to normal. I shall never return to Hungary again.

I think the most insulting act of all was the fact that the tombstones were stolen from the Jewish graves, the names ground off and the stones resold to the Gentiles. It was not bad enough that the Jews of Szikszó were deported to death camps; the people of the town want to erase our history there. This was brought painfully home to me when I took my grandchildren Amara and Brett to the Jewish cemetery to visit the grave of my grandfather so that they could honour him. His tombstone was gone, stolen. I noticed that most of the other tombstones were missing as well. Several years later I learned from a friend of mine from Szikszó now living in London, the full story of what happened to our tombstones. There is no greater act of disrespect for a people than dishonouring their dead.

# 2

# Auschwitz

My father had a very close friend called Lazar Rothschild (no relation to the German banking family of the same name). Lazar Rothschild was one of the most amazing men I ever met and as things transpired he would become a second father to me. I always referred to him as Rothschild Bácsi, which loosely translated means Uncle Rothschild. (It is a shortened form of the Hungarian word for uncle: *nagybácsi*.) It was common in Hungary at that time to refer to close family friends of my parents' generation in that fashion as a sign of respect. In the case of Rothschild Bácsi, I also meant it to signify how much I loved and respected the man and, as we shall see, how important he was to my life.

One of Rothschild Bácsi's sons, László, whose nickname in Hungarian was Laci, was about three years older than me and he was one of my friends. As I mentioned in the previous chapter, he attended *cheder* with me. He was the other kid in my class who stood up to the bullies with me and was ready to take on our tutor when he threatened to beat us. Following the war Laci moved to Israel and then to Canada, where he Canadianized his name to Leslie. But I always referred to him as Laci.

The Rothschild family lived about two kilometres outside of town, where Mr Rothschild had a water-powered flourmill on a canal next to the Hernad River. Mr Rothschild was friendly with the chief of police of Szikszó, and the day before the roundup of the Jews was to take place, he was told by the chief not to be at home. His friend didn't want to have to arrest and deport Mr Rothschild and his family of five children.

Early in the morning of the 17 April 1944, Mr Rothschild got his family out of their house just minutes before the police arrived. They all hid in a ditch not far from the house. Like me, my friend Laci had a dog, and the dog was with them in the ditch. Laci had to choke his dog to death because it was doing what all dogs do when they sense a threat – it started to bark.

Once the police had left his land, Mr Rothschild and his family made their way to a town on the far side of the Hernad River. He went to a farmer he knew and asked to be allowed to hide out on the farm for a time. The farmer refused this request, as the penalty for hiding a Jew was death. However, Mr Rothschild had a gun and he told the farmer that they *would* be staying there. Mr Rothschild and his wife and his five children did stay on the farm for a little while.

They knew better than to stay too long, however, and they were able to sneak into town and take the train to Budapest. Once in Budapest, Mr Rothschild managed to place two of his three sons with Raoul Wallenberg. Wallenberg was the Swedish diplomat stationed in Budapest who bought and rented homes that he turned into safe houses for Jewish children. Since these homes were owned by the Swedish government and thus had diplomatic immunity, neither the Nazis nor the Hungarian government could invade them.

Mr Rothschild took his two daughters, aged nine and eleven, to a convent. He somehow managed to get the girls placed there without letting it be known that they were Jewish. But before he left them he gave each of them a *siddur*, a Jewish prayer book, so that they could pray. It was obviously important to him that his daughters remember their Jewishness. The girls hid the prayer books under their mattresses. Unfortunately, the nuns discovered the books and, instead of protecting the girls, they turned them over to the authorities. The girls were taken away to the Jewish ghetto in Budapest. The ghetto was a gated area segregated from the rest of the city and surrounded by barbed wire. Once in the ghetto it was impossible to get out.

The Hungarian Arrow Cross, like their Nazi counterparts, had an anti-Semitic philosophy and a stereotypical view of what a Jew looked like. Since Mr Rothschild didn't look like their vision of a Jew, he was able to get papers as a member of the Arrow Cross. He grew a moustache to make himself look more like a typical Hungarian and it was that disguise that saved him. Laci, my friend and his oldest son, was disguised as his valet and in that role he too was able to survive the war. Mr Rothschild used his disguise to save as many Jews as he could.

The deportation of Jews started in the countryside, and our region, being the part of Hungary that was closest to Auschwitz, was one of the first, if not the first, to experience the expulsion. Jews of Budapest were not deported in large numbers because it was late in the war and because the Partisans had bombed the railway in certain strategic locations, making it impossible to transport Jews out of Budapest and the surrounding area. Instead, the Arrow Cross would round up groups of Jews, take them to the Danube River, force them to remove their shoes and shoot them. This was the tragic fate of Mr Rothschild's daughters. And so the Blue Danube, made famous by Johann Strauss II, ran red with Jewish blood.

Mr Rothschild was part of the Arrow Cross group that brought those Jews to the riverbank for annihilation. Thus, he found a way to warn many of them and get them to walk in a different direction away from the river, escaping certain death. He saved countless people in that way at great risk to himself. Had Rothschild Básci been caught helping people to escape he would have been killed on the spot.

After the war Mr Rothschild was put into jail because he was prepared to testify in court against Hungarians who collaborated with the Nazis. Many of these Nazi collaborators and Arrow Cross members became part of the Communist government in Hungary after the war. In a way he was lucky to be in jail because others who risked their lives to save Jewish people, men such as Wallenberg, were deported to Russia and never heard from again. During the chaos of the Revolution of 1956 Mr Rothschild got out of jail and made his way to Israel, where Laci then lived. From there they emigrated to New York and then to Toronto. Mr Rothschild's wife, who, along with her brothers, survived the war in the Budapest ghetto, died while he was in prison.

My family's experiences were very different from those of the Rothschilds, but no less tragic. We reported to the city hall as directed. We only knew that we were being removed from Szikszó but we were not told where we were going. The rumour was – and this turned out to be true – that we were to be taken to a ghetto in some other city. The ghetto we were taken to was in the town of Kassa (Košice), some seventy-two kilometres to the north of Szikszó and today part of Slovakia. Like all the other ghettos in Nazi-occupied Europe, the ghetto in Kassa was closed off from the rest of the town and surrounded by barbed wire. The system in place at that time allotted so many people per square metre of living space, and families who had homes were forced to take in the people that the Nazis deported to the ghetto. My family was assigned to live with a lawyer and his wife in their apartment. I remember them as being very nice to us. However, we only stayed with them for two or three weeks. I have no idea what became of them.

We were then told that we would be taken to a new ghetto located in a former brick factory a short distance out of town. This was because so many Jews were coming into the town from the surrounding areas that Kassa couldn't handle them all. The factory was more or less empty. The section in which we were placed was an open area where the bricks were set out for drying. That part of the factory had a roof but no walls; it was open on all four sides. It was May so the weather was warm and the lack of protection from the elements was not a serious problem. But before we could turn the factory into a sort of makeshift living area we had to move the bricks, which were spread out over most of the available floor space. We were lined up in a work chain and we passed the bricks from person to person until we had freed up a space large enough to accommodate us.

Large amounts of straw were brought into the factory and we were allowed to take as much as we needed to make beds. At first we had no idea why we had been taken to this factory, but it wasn't long before we understood the reason. The factory was located on a railroad siding. Most of the holding areas to which the Nazis deported the Jews when they were taken from ghettos were in brick factories because they all had railroad sidings and were situated outside of town so the townspeople couldn't see

how the Jews were being treated. It was very easy for the Nazis
to build a barbed wire fence around a brick factory, thus creat-
ing a prison.

After we had been in the brick factory for a couple of weeks, a
freight train pulled up to the factory and we were herded like animals into railway boxcars. The Hungarian police pushed so many
of us into each car that they had to use large poles, actually beams
held crosswise, to shove us into them.

Again, we had no idea where we were being taken. It was
rumoured that, because of the war, workers were needed and that
once we got to wherever we were going the conditions would be
better. The rumours must have been generated by the Nazis
because they always held the promise of something better; that
there would be no problem once we got to the end of our journey.
Of course these were all Nazi lies, told to keep us submissive and
dependent. If we had known what awaited us, there is the strong
likelihood that we would have rebelled, for what did we have
to lose?

In the days before we were loaded onto the train we were told
that we would be allowed to take water and whatever food we had
with us. We were able to correspond with Mr Mata, our partner in
the farm who owned the pigs, and he found a way to send us
parcels of food that we took with us on the train. We still had the
cookies that my mother had baked, the ones with the jewelry concealed in them.

Once we had been stuffed into the cars, the train started to
move. But the train didn't move at a consistent rate. It would move
slowly and then speed up, and then slow down again. Inside the
cars, conditions were intolerable. By then it was summer, and it
was hot, with barely any room to move. It was impossible to jump
off the train to escape. Each car had one little window but it was
covered with barbed wire.

Periodically the train would stop and the doors to the boxcar in
which we were imprisoned would be opened. At one of these stops
a Nazi functionary told us to put our watches and jewelry into a
bucket that he would hand into the car. We were warned that if
they found any jewelry on our persons or in our belongings that

we had not put into the bucket we would be shot on the spot, so it was better to hand over our possessions then and there. We took a chance and kept the cookies in the backpacks we carried with us but we had to leave all our belongings, including the cookies with the jewelry in them, on the train when we got to Auschwitz.

Following this we were once again crammed into our stinking, crowded, rolling prison and the train started to move. We still had no idea about our destination or what would happen to us once we reached it.

After a couple of days of this we reached our final stop. The Nazis timed our arrival to be in the darkness of night to induce in us an additional level of fear. The doors of our boxcar prisons were unlocked and we were instructed to get out of the train. To say we were frightened is an understatement. Even all these years later it is difficult to find words to express my total sense of despair and terror – and I'm sure my grandmother, my parents and my sister, along with all the others stuffed into all those fetid boxcars felt the same way. Fear has the power to numb and it was feeling thus – numb with fear – that we followed the orders our Nazi captors barked at us.

My mother spoke some German and some Yiddish and she was able to have brief whispered conversations with the inmates who boarded the train car to move us out. We were told to leave our belongings behind and disembark. The inmates who got us out of the train were Polish Jews who had been in the camp for some time.

In Yiddish, my mother asked one of these people, "What is going on? Where are we?" The inmate, indicating me with a slight movement of his head, asked my mother in a whisper, "How old is he?" She told him I was twelve. The inmate said, "He should say he's seventeen." "And what about my daughter?" she asked. The *häftling* (the Nazis used the German word when referring to the inmates of concentration camps and we were expected to do the same) didn't answer. He walked away.

After we got off the train our possessions were transferred onto trucks and taken to a warehouse somewhere in the camp. For reasons that I only learned much later, the warehouse where they stored the possessions they took from arriving Jews was referred to as Canada, because it was a source of great abundance.

Women were told to go to one side and men to the other. As we were being removed from the train and sent to our respective lines, the rumour was that family members would be able to see each other every second day. I can't speculate as to the purpose of these lies, other than to keep us docile and easy to manage, but they were another form of Nazi cruelty – as if more was needed; our situation was more than frightening enough. For the first time in our lives, because we now knew better than to believe the lies of our captors, my sister and I had the feeling to hug one another. Our childhood sibling rivalry was no match for the love we felt for one another in that desperate situation.

My father and I said goodbye to my mother and Marika, and some part of me believed that we would see each other again. We went one way, and mother and Marika went the other. We never saw them again.

The lines moved quickly; the Nazis used vicious, barking dogs to keep the line moving. It was dark, confusing, and terrifying. The train was emptied of all but the most elderly of us. Those who could not walk were told to remain on the train and that they would be taken to some unknown destination by transport. My grandmother too was told to stay on the train. We never saw her again.

The camp guards and the barking dogs herded us to a place where there were bright lights. As we were being marched along a path, I saw that there was a ditch running alongside the road. I looked down. To my horror, I saw babies crawling in the ditch. I asked my father what was going on. "Those bastards," he responded. "We are going to kill them." He was so angry. I think that his anger at what he saw and at was happening to his family overpowered his fear. That's the kind of man he was: strong.

We got to a place where we were told to get undressed but to keep our shoes and socks under our arm and walk one by one through a narrow door. On the other side of the door there was an officer with a stick who pointed at each person as they walked by him and indicated that they were to go to either the left or the right. At that time I didn't speak Yiddish but I did speak some German so I understood what was being said. But I didn't pay any attention to the orders; I stuck as close to my father as I could and followed him. Each time we went through a selection process at the camp, my father always walked ahead of me and I followed as closely behind him as possible. Things happened so quickly that we didn't have a chance to realize exactly what was taking place but I was determined not to be separated from my father.

We were moved into a room where there were men holding clippers. They cut off the hair from our heads, our pubic areas and our underarms. I was too young at that point in my life to have much in the way of body hair but my survival instinct kicked in and I did my best to look older by standing as tall as I could and by wrinkling my forehead. Every time I saw a Nazi officer I would wrinkle my forehead.

Following the process of having our hair shorn, a *häftling* daubed our private parts and underarms with a dirty cloth that had been soaked in some kind of anti-lice substance. After this procedure we were moved into another area, again manned by *häftlings* who had been there for a year or two, and we were given a uniform according to our size. We were allotted underwear, pants, a jacket and a hat, all of which were striped.

Following this we were herded to the barracks that would serve as our sleeping quarters. The one-storey building was a dormitory that held bunk beds in three tiers. The dormitories were extremely crowded and most of us could not stretch out to lie down. We had to sit between another prisoner's legs, leaning against his chest. This was the only way we were able to rest for a few hours.

The next morning we were taken to the tattoo area. Each of us was given a number on a slip of paper and directed to a table where there was a prisoner with what looked like a ballpoint pen but was a tattoo needle and ink. These needles were used on prisoner after prisoner and never cleaned.

As a result of being tattooed with an unclean needle, my arm became infected. It was swollen and very, very painful. When I complained about this to another of the prisoners, a Gentile inmate, he told me, "Shut up and don't complain. You're lucky." "What do you mean I'm lucky?" I asked. "If you didn't have a tattoo you wouldn't be here!" he said. It was an odd way to conceive of luck, but I suppose he was right. But this didn't help with the soreness, and I was in terrible pain for days.

I was tattooed with number A 10,440. This number was also stamped on a piece of cloth and sewn onto the left breast of our jackets. This job was performed by a group of *häftlings* who knew how to sew. Along with our number, there was an indentifying symbol, a *winkel*, indicating the group to which we belonged: Jews wore a yellow triangle, homosexuals wore a pink one, and political prisoners wore a red one.

The "A" stood for Auschwitz. The date was 28 May 1944.

After we were processed, disinfected, and tattooed, we were massed together in a large area that we learned was called the *Appellplatz*. In a more benign environment it would have been a town square but in Auschwitz it was the area where the arriving prisoners were taken in order to be organized for their incarceration. Because my father was a tall and imposing man, a Nazi officer gave him the job of organizing the prisoners into a column of lines, five across. My father did his best but there was great confusion in the *Appellplatz*. In addition to being afraid, the prisoners wanted to remain with their families and they spoke a variety of languages, which made it hard to get them to understand what was being asked of them. My father did his best but was unable to arrange his fellow prisoners into one line, much less into a column of five lines abreast.

The Nazi officer who had commanded my father to organize the prisoners came up to him and, with no warning, whipped him across his face with his riding crop. I could see that my father, even in his shock and horror, wanted nothing more than to punch the Nazi officer square in the face. I was sickened and terrified but I also witnessed the thought process that flashed across my father's face – the realization that if he gave in to his natural instinct it would be the end of him and likely the end of me. He endured the humiliation in order to remain my protector in the hell that awaited us.

My father and I adjusted to life in Auschwitz, if that's what you can call adapting your life to being in a place that was so hellish that the devil himself would be embarrassed to call it his creation. My father and I stuck close to one another. Even in that degredation he acted as a compassionate and caring father. He gave some of his food to me, saying he was not hungry. I felt bad and didn't

want to take his food; I knew he was starving like the rest of us.
More than sharing his food, though, my father shared his strength
with me. Without him I never would have survived.

There is a passage in *Survival in Auschwitz* by Primo Levi that
movingly describes the sense of inner determination that makes it
possible to survive in that hell. He writes:

> We are slaves, deprived of every right, exposed to every insult,
> condemned to certain death, but we still possess one power,
> and we must defend it with all our strength for it is the last –
> the power to refuse our consent. So we must certainly wash
> our faces without soap in dirty water and dry ourselves on our
> jackets. We must polish our shoes, not because the regulation
> states it, but for dignity and propriety. We must walk erect,
> without dragging our feet, not in homage to Prussian disci-
> pline but to remain alive, not to begin to die.*

As I developed the survival skills necessary for life in Auschwitz
I learned where the babies in the ditch that I saw on my first night
there had came from. Women carrying young children who arrived
at Auschwitz were divided into two groups. Some of the woman
and children were sent to their death upon arrival and the other
group were used as slave labour. The rumour among the inmates
was that from the second group the Nazis selected the women they
considered to be the prettiest to serve as prostitutes. These women
had their children taken from them and those babies were tossed in
the ditch to die.

The sex slaves were kept on the top floor of a three-storey building located to the left of the entrance to the camp. On Sundays the
youth of the camp would gather outside this building and the
women imprisoned in it would throw candies to us. The Nazi soldiers gave these poor women some extra sweets after abusing
them, and the women shared them with us. This was their statement that they still possessed a power to rise above the indignity
they suffered.

* Primo Levi, *Survival in Auschwitz*, trans. Stuart Woolf (New York:
  Touchstone/Simon and Schuster, 1996), 41.

I'm sure every reader has seen photographs of camp survivors – hollow-eyed skeletons, barely alive, draped in ill-fitting prison garb. Starvation was our constant companion, the enemy that never left us, the monster that could never be tamed. There is no way I can think of to describe to a person who has never experienced it how hunger can come to dominate one's life. At Auschwitz food was always on our minds; we woke up hungry and went to sleep hungry. We walked to and from our work hungry. I witnessed children who turned on their parents for an extra ration of bread. I even heard of cases in the camp where a son would kill his father to get his food ration and I heard, also, that fathers would do the same to their sons when driven to extreme hunger. Every one of us thought about food for every conscious second of our lives.

So desperate were we for something to eat that we did everything we could to get a little bit extra. When one of our fellow prisoners died, we left him in his bunk so that we could get the bread meant for him. We left the deceased unreported until the Germans noticed he was dead and had the body removed. The Nazis constructed a world in which everything we held dear was taken from us and in which we were treated like animals. In fact, the animals in the camp were treated with more humanity than we were. So it is not surprising that we had to resort to our baser instincts in order to get enough food to survive.

I've been asked many times why we didn't fight back or find other methods of resistance while we were in the camps. The Nazis very cleverly and with evil intent used hunger as a means of control. They knew that if we were kept close to starvation our main focus would be to acquire food and not to resist their authority. They were indifferent to our suffering and didn't care if we died. They referred to us as *stücke*, the German word for "pieces." They saw us as easily replaceable parts of their slave machine. We were never referred to as a person; every one of us was a *stück*, a piece. They attempted to strip us of our humanity.

Life in Auschwitz was well ordered and well organized. There were rules, a lot of them, and along with the rules there were punishments for each transgression, no matter how seemingly insignificant. When confronted by an officer you had to remove your hat.

If you failed to salute an officer fast enough you were knocked down and kicked. If you stole bread there was another, more serious, punishment, and so on – leading to the ultimate penalty: death by hanging.

We had to appear at the *Appellplatz* at least twice a day. In the morning before we were taken to our job assignments, we were counted by the Nazis and the *kapos. Kapos* were prisoners who held a privileged position in the camp. They were given extra food and warmer clothing in exchange for doing the dirty work of our captors; so it was in their interest to follow and enforce the rules of the camp.

At Auschwitz we were assigned jobs. We were asked what our trade had been or what we were capable of doing. My father and I told them that we knew about horses and farming. My father got a job working in the fields, where there was a potato farm. He was required to do backbreaking work with a pick and shovel. A lesser man would not have been able to do the work that my father did on a daily basis. The rule for survival at Auschwitz was simple: if you were unable to work you died.

Included in my father's work detail were another father and son from Szikszó. They were rounded up at the same time as we were and travelled on the same train to Auschwitz. The son was several years older than me, about nineteen or twenty. Their family name was Gutman. In the evening when we returned from work we were marched to the *Appellplatz*, where we were once again counted to ensure that there had been no escapes.

The Nazis insisted that when we entered the gates of Auschwitz upon returning from work – the gates with the sign above them that stated *Arbeit Macht Frei* – that we march with military precision. The *kapos* would bark out the orders *links, rechts, links* – left, right, left. The camp orchestra made up of inmates played martial music that was broadcast over the PA system to accompany our march.

Most punishments and all hangings were administered in the *Appellplatz*. Hangings were scheduled for early in the morning at the time of our daily roll call. On days when a hanging was to take place before we were taken to our work sites, we would be taken to the *Appellplatz* where scaffolding had been brought in for the express purpose of hanging *häftlings* who had tried to escape. In order to demonstrate the consequences of attempting to escape, we were made to watch these poor souls being put to death. Even then, my natural sympathy for my fellow man, my fellow *häftlings*, was overpowered by my hunger. All I could think about was food.

My experience with horses on my father's farm certainly paid off and I got a job working in the stables looking after the riding horses for the SS officers. I had to clean the stables and comb down the horses. If an SS officer wanted to go for a horseback ride I had to get his horse ready for him. That meant making sure that the horse was properly saddled and bridled. I was lucky to be working with horses, as this was less strenuous than working out in the fields. And having access to their food helped stave off my hunger. There was some fodder for the horses stored in the stockroom and I was able to take some of it, mix it with water, and eat it. We weren't supposed to do this but I did it anyway. I'm sure there would have been a severe punishment if I had been caught – but luckily I wasn't.

Problems arose when it came to cleaning the horses. Most people don't know that horses have dandruff. I was required to remove the dandruff with a brush and a scraper. I had to collect the dandruff in the scraper and make lines of dandruff on the floor of the stable to indicate to the overseer that I was doing my job properly. But after a while there wasn't enough dandruff to make the number of lines that the foreman, the *kapo*, a Polish Jew, expected of me. I was weak and tired and could only scrape off so much dandruff. The *kapo* in the stable was not a nice guy. In order for him to retain his position of authority – and his survival depended on this – he had to prove to his Nazi masters that he had no sympathy for the prisoners, the *häftlings*, in his charge. When he saw that I wasn't getting enough work done to satisfy him he put me on report. I didn't have the energy to meet his demands.

Being put on report meant that the *kapo* gave you a slip of paper with your number on it that you had to take to the administration office. The Nazis were as fanatical about record keeping as they were about everything else. We all knew that if we were put on report it was bad news – that there would be a punishment of some kind. And I knew that some people who were put on report had disappeared.

I was in a group of six or seven people from various work groups who were going to the office to register with our numbers. If any of us was taken away by a guard, we would likely never be seen again. While we were in line an ss officer came by, and we expected the worst. But he suddenty asked me, "Can you ride a bike?" "*Ja wohl!*" I replied. The officer took me out of line and told me I was to teach his son how to ride a bike.

So I spent the next two days running after a German kid, teaching him how to ride a bike. The boy was about six, and I taught him to ride a bike in the way that all kids learn how to do it. I held the seat and ran as he pedalled until he learned how to keep his balance and ride on his own. I never learned the name of my young student; nor did I know the name of his father. In fact, even though I tried to talk to the boy he wouldn't talk to me. He had probably been told not to have any contact with me beyond the bike-riding lessons. But because I had the job teaching him to ride his bike, I never had to report to the administrative office, and this surely saved my life.

After these bike-riding lessons, I was assigned to work in the stock room, cleaning and repairing the picks and shovels. These implements were used by the men who worked on the farm and they came back every day covered in mud. I was part of a crew who cleaned the picks and shovels daily and were also responsible for making repairs to them when necessary. This meant repairing or replacing a broken handle and similar types of small improvements. There was no shortage of equipment, so while we were working on those that needed cleaning and repair, other implements were available for use. Each morning we gave out the tools to the guys who worked in the fields; my father was one of them.

In Auschwitz, among other privations, we had no way of keeping our teeth clean. At some point I developed a terrible toothache, an abscess. Obviously there was no hope of dental care so I went to see the veterinarian who worked with the horses. The vet was another of the Polish prisoners – probably a political prisoner. I asked him to help me by removing the infected tooth. He agreed, but told me that if anyone came by I had to get out of sight. As he was poking around in my mouth, jerking my tooth back and forth, he must have seen someone coming because he suddenly told me to disappear. I took off and hid. After the Nazi officer left, I went back to the vet and he completed the process of removing my tooth.

The *kapo* in charge of the stock room was not Jewish; nor was he a camp employee. He was a political prisoner, probably a left-winger of some description. Many of the other prisoners working in the stockroom were leftists and most of them were Polish. This *kapo* was a decent guy. Since most of the people who worked with me in the stockroom were Polish, they spoke their native language to one another. I have always been interested in learning languages and I pick them up quickly. It didn't take me long to be able to speak a bit of Polish to the other prisoners. I wasn't fluent but I could speak enough to make myself understood and the other guys liked it that I made an effort to speak their language. The *kapo* especially liked me for that reason.

The work was hard but I could do it. In fact, one of the survival skills I developed in Auschwitz, a skill that would stay with me for the rest of my life, was to tell myself, "If this other guy can do it then so can I." This is one of the beliefs that kept me going during this period.

The farm where my father worked was in a heavily guarded area outside the camp. Every morning I would walk with my father a distance of some four kilometres as far as the stockroom and he would walk a little farther to the farming area. In the evening I would walk back to the barracks with him. This lent a bit of normality to our lives. In Szikszó it had been part of our routine to go to the farm together.

Hunger never left me while I was a prisoner in Auschwitz. It is impossible to explain what it was like to live with the gnawing feeling of near starvation day in and day out. It felt like I had an angry sharp-clawed animal constantly scratching at my innards. If the Nazis had had a system whereby an inmate could exchange a finger for as much food as he could eat, I would have given up a finger or two without hesitation. My last thought – a hallucination really – at night before falling asleep was about food, and while sleeping I dreamt about it. It led me to do some extraordinary things.

All my life, even as a kid, I've been a risk taker. At Auschwitz I took a risk in order to get extra food for my father and myself. Our barracks was located almost directly across from the kitchen. The living area was completely surrounded by fencing, with towers and search lights strategically placed at intervals so the guards could make certain that no one tried to escape or leave their barracks. Auschwitz was always well illuminated, but the guards in the towers also had a searchlight that slowly rotated to give them a better view of the camp. There was a 10:00 p.m. curfew and after the curfew the searchlight moved in a circle so the guards could see if anyone was out of their barracks. If they saw someone they would shoot to kill.

I figured out that the guards' attention was where the searchlight shone. I calculated that while the searchlight was arced away from the stretch between our barracks and the kitchen area, I could run across the open space and climb over the gate and into the kitchen area without being seen. There, in the kitchen yard, I found piles of potato skins. The Nazi officers and the other camp staff ate a lot of potatoes but they had prisoners peel them first. So the skins were left in the yard. (I never understood why they bothered to peel the potatoes – it would have been simpler and more nutritious to wash them, cook them, and eat them with the skins.) In any event, I would stuff my shirt with potato skins and when the searchlight again circled away from the open area between the kitchen and the barracks I would run back. My father and I ate the potato skins raw while in our beds.

My father thought I was crazy to take this risk. He worried that I would be seen and be shot. It was normal for a parent to worry about his child. But it was the same spirit that made me want to ride a horse that no one else could ride that made me take the risk to get more food. I don't think my father fully understood this. Also, I was at an age where kids take chances and even though I was in the worst place on earth I couldn't completely deny my personality.

One night, while I was out on the potato skin hunt, my father heard shots from outside our barracks and he was certain that I had been shot. But the shooting was not in the part of the open field where I was running. In another part of the camp, close to our barracks, some kids went to the fence that separated the women's section from that of the men. They were looking for their families. The guards saw them and shot them – for the guards it was nothing, they had absolutely no regard for our lives. I kept on stealing potato skins.

On another night, just as I was getting ready to run across the road to our barracks an office shouted "Halt!" in German. I looked around and saw an SS officer. I thought, "Oh, I'm in trouble!" I was sure I would be killed. He shouted at me in German, "What are you doing there?" I told him that I worked in the kitchen and that I had forgotten something. He yelled, "You're not supposed to be outside, you dirty Jew." I could tell that he was drunk. He took out his gun and shouted, "Get back to your barracks." I hoped that he was too drunk to shoot straight so I ran back in a zigzag pattern so as not to get shot. He didn't shoot. That was the last time I went to the kitchen to steal potato skins. I never told my father the reason I stopped, but he was relieved that I did.

This was another survival skill I learned at Auschwitz: to know when *not* to take a risk. Auschwitz was the worst possible place to learn this lesson as the consequences for failing to learn it could mean certain death. On the other hand, once the lesson is learned under these circumstances it stays with you for life.

During the summer of my incarceration I remember watching with envy as the birds flew overhead. I saw that they could fly out of the camp and I wished I was a bird and could do the same.

In Auschwitz we didn't know from week to week whether we would live or die. Every Wednesday was shower day. When we went to the showers we had to take off our clothes and hold them under our arm when we went into the shower room. We believed that because we worked very hard, we would have a real shower and wouldn't be eliminated.

But regardless of how hard we worked, there was a periodic selection process involved with the weekly showers. From time to time a Nazi officer was stationed at the narrow door we had to pass through to get to the showers and he would cull out the prisoners he considered to be weak. As usual, there were commands of *links*, *rechts*, with one line getting a real shower and the other being put to death. There was no shortage of replacements for the inmates that were killed because trains filled with prisoners were arriving all day and all night.

I didn't take the chance of being seen by the Nazi inspector. I stuck as close to my father as possible and we invariably went in the direction of the shower room – away from the gas chamber.

When we went into the showers we were issued small bars of soap, only a little larger than a pat of butter. They were impressed with the letters RJF, which stood for the words *Rein jüdisches Fett*. It was rumoured that the soap was made from the body fat of murdered Jews. This small piece of soap brought the most terrible and painful thoughts to my mind. Was I washing with soap made from my mother and little sister? Were they hugging when they were choking to death in the gas chamber? Or were they put into ovens and burned alive? Nazi evil didn't even allow us to have a pleasant memory of our murdered loved ones in their final minutes. These thoughts created in me an anger that took many years to recede. While in Auschwitz I did my best to suppress these thoughts; I didn't want despair to conquer hope. I knew instinctively that if I gave up the hope of being reunited with my mother and sister it would be difficult, if not impossible, to survive.

We had to live with the unrelenting fear of being put to death and there is no question that the desire and effort to survive consumed most of our energy. Beyond this surreal cloud of terror and uncertainty, daily life in Auschwitz didn't vary much from day to day. I took strength from my father. His constant words to me were, "Son, once we get out of here, we're going to kill them." He was very angry and his anger gave him strength. He never doubted that we would survive. Or perhaps he did have his doubts – he would not have been human if he didn't – but he never let on to me that he was anything but angry, and I drew energy and comfort from this. I felt that if the guy working next to me could survive then I could as well.

My father was a good man. In his real life, the life he had made for himself and his family before being sent to Auschwitz, he would, without fail, extend a helping hand to those in need. He made a point of treating everyone – employees, colleagues, friends, and family – fairly. The Nazis did their best to crush that goodness out of him but they never succeeded.

Many of the camp guards were from the Ukraine and they were well known to be the cruellest of the guards. All the guards had sticks and they enjoyed hitting us with them. There was a Ukrainian fellow who was one of the most sadistic. He had a dog that he called "Man" – that was the name he gave to the dog – "Man." He trained the dog to be mean and to attack us. He would tell his dog "Man" to attack the "Dogs" – that was his name for Jews – "Dogs." And the dog would attack us by going for our private parts. The dog was trained to attack Jews in that way. Dogs are naturally loyal and loving creatures; they will follow their master's bidding, but on their own they are not malevolent. It takes a special kind of evil to abuse the animal's natural devotion and transmogrify it into something hateful. Nazism infected all those who came under its spell with a very special malignancy – even the dogs.

The weather got colder as winter approached. The cold weather didn't mean that there was a letup in our work, but we were given some warmer used clothing that came from the warehouse called "Canada." The cold weather just made our work harder. Every Sunday afternoon we had to take the horses out to graze on an island. In the spring and summer it was not too difficult to walk across the river because the water level was low and even though we got wet, the warm weather dried us. In the rainy season the water level rose and, of course, the water got a lot colder. We weren't allowed to sit on the horses. We had to walk them across the river as we did in the warmer seasons. Not only did the river get deeper and colder but it also got wider. We had to take off our shoes, tie them together by the laces and sling them around our necks. We held the reins of two horses in each hand to lead them across the river to the island.

In November of 1944 I became ill from malnutrition and from having to cross an almost frozen river with the horses. I started to run a fever but I did my best to work for as long as I could because I didn't want to be separated from my father. But by mid-December my fever was so high that it was impossible for me to work and my father had to take me to the camp infirmary.

The Emergency section of the infirmary was for minor injuries; the doctors would patch you up and send you back to work. When we arrived at the Emergency section, the doctor in charge was a prisoner, a Czech doctor named Alex Grunwald. He diagnosed me with pneumonia and I had water in my lungs. He used a big needle to draw a lot of water from my lungs and assigned me to a bed. When the German doctor came to the ward, Dr Grunwald told him I was getting better and that I would be sent back to work very soon. But he never did send me back to work. He always found a way to prolong my stay. One of the things he did was to give me pills that caused me to run a fever and he continued to tell the German doctor I would be better in a few days. Somehow Dr Grunwald managed to keep me in the hospital through December and into January. Even in that soulless slice of hell, my father never stopped being a loving and nurturing man. He came to see me every night.

We could tell that the Russian Army was getting closer. There were a number of prisoners who had served in the army during the First World War and they could recognize by the sound of the gunfire how far the fighting was from camp. There would be gunfire for a while and then the guns would fall silent so we didn't know if the Russians were advancing or retreating.

Meanwhile the Germans started to evacuate the camp and move prisoners to other camps. The Nazis ordered everyone who could walk to report to a central location and to form a line. But Dr Grunwald would not allow me to leave the infirmary. He obviously had some authority and he informed the guard, also a prisoner, not to permit me to be removed from the facility.

That night my father did not come to see me. Those of us in the infirmary could see out the window that the Nazis were getting all the inmates who could walk into a column, five abreast. This evacuation of Auschwitz was what became known as the *Todesmarsch* – the Death March. I saw my father from the window of the infirmary as he marched by and we waved to one another. At that moment I still believed that, once the war was over, I would be reunited with him and the rest of my family in Szikszó. I didn't know it then, but that was the last time I saw my father,

The Gutmans, the other father and son from Szikszó, were on the Death March with my father and it was from them that I found out, on my return to Szikszó, what had happened to my father. The last words he spoke were to Mr Gutman and his son. His words, straightforward and to the point, spoke of the heartbreak he felt at leaving me behind. He said, "Now I have lost everything. I lost my wife and my daughter and now I have lost my son." He had no desire to continue on the march. His loss was too great. So, having said what he said, he fell out of line. When an inmate did not hold to his position in the line the Nazis shot him in the head. That is what happened to my father. A Nazi soldier shot him in the head and left his body at the side of the road.

When I learned of the fate of my father I was enveloped by feelings of remorse and sadness. I wondered then, and I wonder now, if things would have been different if we had been together on the *Todesmarsch*. Would we have been able to encourage one another to take the next step and then the next one and so on until we made it to safety? My grief at losing my father on the Death March has never left me.

I knew that when my father was marched out of camp his life was at risk. My sense of loss then was intense. When I heard what actually happened to him my sorrow was magnified. It upset me then and it upsets me to this day that there is no tombstone or grave at which I can mourn my father – the man who gave me life and who saved my life on more occasions than I can count.

I had a friend at the camp who also used to work with the horses; I worked with the riding horses and he worked with the working horses, the horses used to plough the fields. He was a little older than me, about seventeen or eighteen years old. His name was also George, George Torok. He was a strong kid who had been a gymnast before being brought to the camp. At Auschwitz, there were times, usually on Sundays, when the guards arranged for the inmates to entertain them. George was part of these entertainments. He performed some of his gymnastic exercises. I assisted him by holding the ropes he climbed and doing other small chores to help him. If the guards liked the performance they would throw us a piece of bread in the same way that you would throw a peanut to a performing monkey. My friend would share his bread with me.

In order to survive at Auschwitz it was critical to have friends. People like George would share their extra food with their friends. I shared the potato skins that I stole from the kitchen with my father and with the people with whom we were friends. These small acts of kindness were repeated over and over again. But there were some guys who were loners, who did not form bonds of friendship with their fellow prisoners. These people had an even tougher time than the rest of us and likely did not survive.

My friend George found out from my father that I was in the infirmary and from time to time he came to visit me. On one of his visits he took a chance and stayed overnight. Under normal circumstances in the camp this would have been a very dangerous thing to do. But we knew the Nazis were in a panic owing to the approach of the Russian Army and we believed that in the resulting chaos the rules were not being enforced.

The next morning we discovered that there were no longer any Nazis in the camp. They had all moved out. We went and broke into the kitchen stockroom to get some food. I remember very clearly that there was a lot of pudding mix, so we made pudding. This went on for a couple of days. It was a time of great confusion. We took advantage of the disappearance of the Nazis and broke into the warehouse where the clothing was kept. I got myself a nice pair of boots and a warm coat from "Canada."

After about a week the Nazis returned. Three trucks filled with soldiers rolled into the camp and we were forced out of the various places we had broken into. At the moment of their return, a bunch of us were in the stockroom of the kitchen foraging for food. The soldiers started shooting at us and we all took off running. I just made it around the corner of the stockroom to safety and so I didn't get shot. But many of the prisoners were not as fast as I was and did get murdered. A Dutch-Jewish doctor with whom we were friendly couldn't run as fast as we could and so he didn't make it around the corner of the building safely. He was just a few paces behind my friend George. George made it to safety but the doctor was shot.

Following some kind of atavistic impulse to return to the only home we had at Auschwitz, we had returned to our quarters. The Nazi soldiers came in bearing machine guns and we were ordered out. My instinct told me not to follow their orders and I jumped out of the window into the snow. I wasn't going to go down the stairs, I feared a trap. It would have been too easy for the Nazis to shoot us as we came out of the building. My friend George went down the stairs and he was put in a line facing a machine gun. They brought the people from the buildings out into the open area. I was hiding in the snow where I had landed after my jump.

The Nazis had everyone line up in single file. Dr Grunwald was in the line along with everyone else. I feared that if I was spotted, I would be shot immediately, so when I saw my friend George I went to stand beside him. All the *häftlings* were lined up and there was a machine gunner placed approximately every twenty-five metres. It was pretty clear to all of us that we were about to be shot. I estimate that there were about three hundred of us in that line of prisoners. George and I bravely shook hands and said our good-byes, that it had been nice to know one another.

I decided that when the soldiers started shooting I was going to fall down and pretend to be dead. The soldiers in the trucks were talking on their two-way radios while the soldiers manning the machine guns kept us in their sights. It became apparent that the soldiers were waiting for orders. After a couple of hours the soldiers who were operating the radios signalled that all of them were to evacuate. The soldiers who were at the machine guns loaded their weapons onto the trucks as they started to move. The soldiers not already on the trucks had to run after them to ensure that they wouldn't be left behind. They jumped onto the moving vehicles as they drove away. That was the last we saw of them and I remember clearly that it was a Thursday night. Two days later, on Saturday, the Russian Army came into the camp.

Our first inkling that the Russian Army had arrived at the camp came when, from our window, we noticed something moving in the snow. We saw one man, then a couple of men, all dressed in white moving through the snow. It looked to us as if the snow itself was moving. One of the men stood up and waved, and within

ten minutes there were hundreds of Russian soldiers in the camp
mingling with the surviving prisoners. Many of the Russian soldiers were Jews who spoke Yiddish. The language we inmates
spoke in Auschwitz was Yiddish – it was there that I learned the
language. Thus we were able to communicate with the Russians.
George Torok was a Czech and spoke some Russian. He was able
to communicate in their language with the soldiers who did not
speak Yiddish.

We were overjoyed to see the Russian soldiers and greeted them
with cheers of thanks and hugs. We cried as we embraced our liberators and for the first time since I arrived in Auschwitz my tears
were tears of joy. The soldiers, especially the Jews among them,
were also overcome with emotion and they responded to our hugs
and tears with hugs and tears of their own.

The first thing I did with my friend George and some other guys
was to look for some Nazi soldiers. We were hell-bent on revenge
and we wanted to kill them. We actually found some Nazis who
were hiding from the Russians and we were about to club them to
death with some bricks we had picked up while conducting our
search, when some Russian soldiers appeared. They stopped us and
took the Nazis away.

The next thing we did was to once again raid the stock room
that held the food. We took the food to our beds and ate as much
as we wanted for the first time since we had been taken from our
home in Szikszó. It didn't take the Russians long to set up a food
distribution system for us so that it was given out on a more equi-
table basis.

The Russian soldiers did more than ensure that we were properly fed. They also made certain that we had warmer clothing. Our
striped concentration camp garb was completely insufficient to
keep us warm. We found another storeroom, where the Nazis kept
the clothing they took from the prisoners as they arrived. Each of
the jackets in the storeroom had a red line four inches wide paint-
ed on it. If any of the inmates had been able to steal one of these
jackets and attempt to wear it to escape he would be spotted
immediately because of the red stripe. In all likelihood anyone
attempting to escape would be shot on the spot. The red line on
the clothing served as a target.

By and large the Russian soldiers were very sympathetic to us and they did their best to try to make our lives bearable while they worked out what to do with us. The only time they were not kind to us was when they were drunk. And because the soldiers were given vodka daily they were drunk a good deal of the time. I guess the vodka provided the extra measure of bravery they needed to fight the Germans on the Russian front.

As we were adjusting to our freedom, a cousin of mine, Tibor, who was eighteen years old at the time and who had been too weak to go on the Death March, came to the infirmary. He had been imprisoned in another area of the camp. He had problems with his legs so he was lucky to be alive.

I, too, was lucky to be alive and I owe my life, in those final days of imprisonment to Dr Grunwald. He kept me in the infirmary and spared me being taken on the Death March. I was still weak from my pneumonia and never would have survived it.

Many years later, when I had begun my new life in Canada, I made efforts to find Dr Grunwald. I checked whatever sources I could. But in the days before the Internet it was difficult to locate people who had passed out of our lives. In 1999 or 2000 I was on a mission with the Canadian Jewish Congress, and we visited Theresienstadt and Israel. While we were in Prague we visited a Jewish centre and I made inquiries to see if anyone knew Dr Grunwald. I was delighted when one of the people at the centre claimed to know a Dr Grunwald as a friend. A short conversation determined that the Dr Grunwald I was seeking was indeed the same man who was their friend. I was told that he had died but that his wife, also a doctor, was still alive and living in Prague.

Her name was Maria Grunwaldova, and I was overjoyed to be able to find her and arrange a visit. She and I spent a pleasant and emotional afternoon together. I told her something of my history, how I had come to know her husband and how deeply grateful I was and would always be for his having saved my life. She told me he had saved many people and those of them that she had been able to meet all told stories similar to mine.

It gave me great pleasure to be able to send Maria Grunwaldova money from the time that I met her until her death. Also, because

Dr Grunwald had saved my life I was able to care for my cousin Tibor. I kept him with me as the Russians took us out of Auschwitz and began the long process of repatriating us.

The date the Russians liberated us was Saturday, 27 January 1945.

# 3

# The Journey Home

I have no way of knowing for sure if the Russian soldiers who liberated Auschwitz had any idea what they would find when they entered the camp. But the liberating army was made up mostly of peasants who were drafted into the army to become soldiers, and it is unlikely they would have had any idea what to expect.

My suspicion is that the officer corps and the higher-ups in the army knew what the Nazis were up to. Hitler's speeches were hardly a secret and the Allies knew he wanted to eliminate the Jews of Europe. Also they had, without a doubt, intelligence sources reporting on the concentration camps and the role the camps played in the Nazis' overall plans. The Allies had the Enigma machine so they knew a lot about the Nazi war effort.

Another fact that led me to believe that the Allied authorities knew all about the death camps is that they did *not* bomb the areas around the camps in any way that would halt the intake of prisoners. They didn't drop bombs on the railway lines or bridges that the Nazis used to deliver Jews to their deaths. They did drop bombs on factories and other installations just outside the camps in furtherance of their war efforts. So they must have known where the camps were in order not to bomb them. Their lack of military support had the effect of ensuring that more Jews were sent to their deaths.*

---

* The Allies knew, or should have known, from both publicly available and private sources of information that the Nazis put their ideology of ridding Europe (and the world) of Jews ahead of all other considerations. Thus, their not bombing the camps allowed the Nazis to continue in their murderous ways.

When Allied aircraft flew overhead, an air raid siren would sound and all the prisoners would have to stop working and report to their barracks or some other indoor place. The Nazis were nervous that if we were outside we would give a signal to the Allies and they would bomb the camp. I was pleased when work was interrupted as it gave me and the other inmates a break from our backbreaking labours. It also meant that the war was nearing an end. As I witnessed the American planes flying overhead, I hoped that the war was truly coming to a conclusion and that I would be reunited with my family.

After the Allies won the war, they claimed that they could not have bombed the camps because their planes didn't have the range to get as far as Auschwitz. I know now, and I knew then, that this was false because I saw their planes flying overhead almost daily. The Allied indifference to the suffering of the Jews had the effect of allowing the Nazis to continue their program of eliminating the Jews of Europe. This, in my opinion, was a doubly shameful act: first, because the Allies knew what was going on in the camps and could have brought an earlier end to the slaughter; and second, because they lied about it after the fact. If the Allies had had the moral integrity to bomb the railway lines and bridges leading to Auschwitz it would have prevented the deaths of my mother and my sister and thousands of others in the crematoria. It angers me to this day that we make heroes of the leaders whose indifference to the suffering of the Jews allowed the ovens of Auschwitz to work at full blast.

The anti-Semitism of the Allied leaders is well known. Canada would not allow any Jewish immigrants into the country. The Americans turned back the MS *St Louis*, a ship containing nine hundred Jewish refugees trying to escape the Holocaust. These and other acts played into the hands of the Nazi war effort to rid Europe of Jews. Because of this, I believe that the Allies knowingly helped in the destruction of European Jewry.

Still, being aware of what was going on in the camps and seeing it firsthand are two very different things. The Russian soldiers were horrified by what they found – hundreds of inmates, Jews from all over Europe and a smattering of political prisoners, mostly Poles, all of whom were dressed in little more than rags and were on the verge of starvation. Those of us who remained were either too sick or too weak to have been taken on the Death March. My friend George was probably the healthiest of us – he was smart enough or just plain lucky to have remained in the infirmary with me.

I was spared the Death March because Dr Grunwald had given me a medicine of some sort to keep my fever high and had repeatedly told the Nazi doctor that I would soon be cured and would be able to go back to work. He kept this subterfuge up for about two weeks. I don't think the Nazi doctor cared about me. He was more concerned with the fact that the Russian Army was closing in on Auschwitz and he wanted to save his own skin.

Dr Grunwald's bravery kept me and several other people who were in the infirmary from going on the Death March, a march I likely would not have survived. I have no way of knowing what would have become of me if I had been on the march. According to the Gutmans, who survived the Death March, barely half of the group survived to reach its destination in western Germany, where they were liberated by the American Army.

Once the Russian soldiers had set up food distribution and completed other organizational chores, they informed us that we would be moved to another camp. They moved us by train to Katowice, a mining town some thirty-five kilometres from the concentration camp. We stayed there for about a month, after which the Russians told us they couldn't take us home until they had proper identification for each of us. I never understood how they thought they could procure such information, considering that we had been stripped of all our belongings and documentation when we entered Auschwitz. But I kept as positive an outlook as possible and hoped they would figure out a solution to that problem before too long.

In the mean time I was enjoying my freedom, limited though it may have been by being stuck in a mining town with nothing to do and nowhere to go. I also still nurtured the hope of being reunited with my family, or as many members of it that were able to survive the camps. When we were taken from our home we made a pact to meet up again in Szikszó after the war. I hoped that other members of the Reinitz clan, and especially my father, mother, and sister, were making their way back there as I was. I still hoped they had somehow survived and that I would see them again.

I have two strong memories of the time I spent at Katowice. The first is that the area of our encampment was very close to a coalmine. There was coal dust everywhere, covering everything in the town. Even the unpaved roads were as black as coal.

My second memory has to do with my warm boots from "Canada," which I found when we raided the stockroom at Auschwitz. I was afraid that if I took them off they would be stolen, so I wore them for three weeks, even going so far as to sleep in them. One night I decided to take the chance of removing them when I went to sleep. I placed them under my head for safety, believing it would be impossible to steal them while I was sleeping on top of them. I was wrong. When I awoke the boots were gone. My cousin Tibor went to the authorities and obtained an old pair of shoes for me. They were neither as warm nor as comfortable as the boots that had been stolen but I had no choice but to wear them. I examined the footwear of everyone I came into contact with, but I never located my boots.

By mid-March of 1945 we were moved again. This time we were taken by train to Czernowitz (Chernivtsi), a city of perhaps half a million people in the province of Bukovina. The city had originally been in the country of Romania. But following the Russian conquest of that area during the war, the border was moved and the city was now in the Ukraine, then a part of the Soviet Union. Czernowitz was a distance of about seven hundred kilometres southeast of Katowice and a hundred kilometres from the Hungarian border. I was very happy to be moving closer to the Hungarian border and I hoped that the next destination would be home.

We were housed in an army barracks in the centre of the city of Czernowitz. There was an active Jewish community in Czernowitz that had never been deported. As soon as the community members learned that a large group of Auschwitz survivors were encamped in their city, they came to our barracks with food. This community did everything they could to look after us.

We were free to leave the barracks of Czernowitz and I took advantage of the opportunity to see something of the city. Once, as I was walking on a street, a woman took hold of me – I mean that literally; she grabbed my arm and wouldn't let go. After a brief conversation in Yiddish during which she confirmed her suspicion that I was a Jew and a survivor, she took me to a store and bought all kinds of food for me. She lived in a small apartment with her husband and her sister, and they insisted that I come to their house every Friday night for Shabbat dinner. Sadly, I've forgotten their name but I'll never forget their kindness.

Even though we were free to come and go as we pleased when we lived in Czernowitz, there was no place to go. Other than my trip to the city and my Friday night dinners, I stuck pretty close to the barracks. I was still with my cousin Tibor and as he had difficulty walking I didn't want to leave him. Tibor was older than me but I was more able to look after him than he was of me.

The population of the camp in Czernowitz included not only people whom the Russians had liberated from Auschwitz but also any soldiers and others they found who could not identify themselves. The camp included many nationalities but there were no Germans. The German prisoners were transported to Russia on a separate train.

Again, the Russian authorities told us that as soon as they got some identification to prove who we were – that we were who we said we were – they would take us home. A group of us approached one of the people in charge who gave us this news, and one of the guys who spoke Russian said, "Mister, we have numbers on our arms." We thought that would prove we were who we said we were, but it didn't help at all.

The winter ended as we were being transported from Auschwitz to Katowice to Czernowitz. The war ended on 5 May 1945, almost a year after my arrival at Auschwitz, and I was impatient to get home. The Russian Army needed the barracks for the soldiers who were returning from the front, so they put us on a train in order to move us to yet another camp. Again, we weren't told where we were going. The Russians had noted our names and our countries of origin while we were in Katowice and told us that they were still waiting for proof of our identity from our native countries, in my case Hungary. At least the Russians discontinued the practice of referring to us by number when they liberated us. They had restored our names to us.

The freight train we were on had upper and lower bunk beds separated by planks of wood. I had learned at Auschwitz always to take the top bed, otherwise you risked getting urinated on at night. The train would sometimes travel a long distance before it stopped. When it stopped at a station we would be given some food, usually soup. Sometimes the train would stop for a day or two. In those cases I would get off the train and look for a farm where I could steal a chicken. I became very adept at chicken stealing and killing. It took me no time at all to catch one and snap its neck.

The Russians took us to the town of Slutsk about seven hundred kilometres northeast of Czernowitz, in Belarus, close to the swamps of Prepit. There is a Yiddish song about the beauty of Slutsk – "Slutsk, oy Slutsk, mayn shtetele" – but my experience of the town was the opposite. It was far from beautiful. Barely one house was left standing in the city! People were living in shacks with tin roofs. The war had obviously devastated the town. But the big army installation was still standing, and that is where we were housed. All in all I estimated there were about 25,000 of us at this point.

Trains full of German soldiers passed through Slutsk. The soldiers were not allowed to get off the train. They were not going to be interned in the army barracks in Slutsk but were heading further north – to work camps.

The barracks in Slutsk was a temporary home to people from all over Eastern and Western Europe – Italians, Greeks, Hungarians, Poles, and Portuguese. I have no idea how the Russians found all these people. I learned later that Primo Levi, the famous Italian scientist and writer whose books chronicled the concentration camp experience, was in Slutsk at the same time as I was there. We arrived there in June of 1945 and remained there until December of that year.

There was little for us to do while we were in Slutsk. There was no work for us so we just hung around wasting time. Somehow we got our hands on some soccer balls and we played soccer. There were some Hungarian and Italian soldiers mixed into the population of Auschwitz survivors, and fights periodically broke out. But they were not serious. We were free to leave the camp but, again, there was nowhere to go so those who left were soon back.

Following our liberation from Auschwitz most of us developed a problem with lice. One of the ways we found to alleviate the boredom while in the camp in Slutsk was to have lice races. We would pull a louse from our underarms or heads, draw a finish line on the floor, and race them.

One of my friends in Slutsk was a tinsmith. There were all kinds of empty tin cans lying around the barracks. He realized that we could flatten the cans and make them into metal sheets by folding the edges of the tin and interlocking the flattened pieces. Once this was done we could make articles, such as bowls out of the sheets of tin. Three or four of us worked on this project. Some of us would scavenge for cans and others would make the tin sheets and shape them into bowls and plates and other products. We turned this into a little business.

By this time I had learned some Russian and we were able to trade these items with some of the local farmers for extra food. The food our liberators fed us was very bland. It was the same every day: cabbage soup and fish, very salty fish. With our business we could procure eggs and milk and other products. In addition to providing us with extra food, our little enterprise gave structure to our lives. It meant that we had a purpose and something to do each day.

We also had another way of getting our hands on more food while we were in Slutsk. We found a potato farm near our camp and we would go and help ourselves to potatoes just before they were ready to be harvested. We would fill up our shirts with potatoes and carry them back to the barracks. We did this at night, of course. It was much too dangerous to try to steal potatoes during the day as there were people working the fields at that time. If we got more potatoes than we could eat, we would trade or sell the remainder.

One night a friend and I went to the field to gather potatoes and we found farmers waiting for us. They knew we had been stealing their crops. They were carrying scythes and clearly intended to kill us for stealing their produce. My friend had been shot earlier and was not in good shape – but he was able to run if necessary. As the two of us ran away, the farmer hurled his scythe at me and almost killed me. I never went back to the farm after that. I decided that the reward was no longer worth the risk.

In October of 1945 we were told that we would be taken home at last – as soon as the Russians could assemble a train. Either they got some kind of proof as to who each of us was or, more likely, they got tired of moving us around Eastern Europe from barracks to barracks, and decided to believe that we were who we said we were. The train they assembled had different cars: boxcars, for the different nationalities: for Romanians, for Serbs, for Hungarians, for Italians, and so on. Again, I made certain to get an upper bunk. As the train got to the country where the occupants of a series of train cars lived, they would be let off the train. It went through Europe, at least as far as Italy, where Primo Levi disembarked. There were a lot of Italians on the train.

It was interesting for me many years later, in 1997, to watch the movie *The Truce*, based on Primo Levi's memoir of the same name. His book and the film chronicled our long journey home while under the charge of the Russians, and included some scenes of our lives in Slutsk.

While we were heading home on the train it was important to get along with each other. Anyone who didn't fit in would have a problem. There was one guy on our car who was full of lice and was always fighting. He paid the price. Once, when the door to the car was open, we threw him off the train without a second thought. I've always had a problem with belligerent people, whether the bully in *cheder* or the pain-in-the-ass on the train.

Whenever the train stopped we used to go out and steal food. We would find homes with little gardens or a chicken or two close to the train station and steal what we could. There was always hot water dripping from the engine so we would find a pot, get some water, build a fire, boil the water and make a sort of chicken and vegetable soup.

Because the trains the Russians used to transport us back to our homes in Europe were boxcars, there was no place to sit. We used to climb onto the tops of the cars and sit up there on the roof, watching the countryside pass us by – a very different experience than we had in the sealed boxcars with a single wire-covered window that took us to Auschwitz. I get nightmares to this day when I think of the things that I did on the tops of the boxcars: we would jump from car to car when the train was stopped – a miscalculation in the distance would lead to a serious fall. And we would stand up on the cars while they were moving. On one occasion I didn't realize until the very last second that we were heading for an overpass. If I hadn't dropped to my stomach, my head would have landed somewhere in Eastern Europe while my body continued the journey west. I decided to be more cautious after that experience.

When the train stopped in Szolnok, the city my mother came from, I went to look for my grandparents and my uncle Dennis. I was taking a chance, because I didn't know how long the train would remain in the station. I couldn't find either my grandfather or grandmother. But when I got to my grandparents' house I met my Uncle Dennis's girlfriend, Terri. She told me that my mother's parents had not survived the war. Dennis, she informed me, had survived and was at work. She told me she would contact Dennis and let him know that I would be heading back to the train station. She would urge him to catch up with me as soon as possible as there was no way of knowing how long the train would remain in Szolnok before it left for Budapest. Obviously Terri was able to get in touch with Dennis because he caught up with me on his bike just before I got to the train station.

For some reason he suggested that I continue on to Budapest and meet him at the home of my great-aunt and great-uncle. He would come and pick me up a couple of days later, he said. I did as he suggested and got back on the train.

I continued on to Budapest, arriving in December 1945. When the train finally pulled into the city, I was so happy to be home – well almost home – that I was dancing on the top of the train like an idiot. I had forgotten my determination to be careful and almost got hit in the head again by an overpass just as we approached the train station.

My joy was based on my belief that my family was alive and that we would be reunited in Szikszó. I had had no word of my family, but as far as I was concerned they must have all survived the horror or incarceration. After all that I had been through, and during the long journey home, I was sustained by the belief that I would soon be with them again and that once we were together we would live happily, putting the horror of the previous couple of years behind us.

I did as my uncle Dennis told me and made my way to my great-uncle's house. This man, my grandfather's brother, was a famous photographer named Komaromi, who before the Revolution had apparently photographed members of the aristocracy. He had also taken some photographs of my family before the war and they are the only photos I have of the four of us. Dennis managed to protect these photographs during the war and he later gave them to me.

I went to the apartment where my great-aunt and great-uncle lived but I didn't get a very warm, or even kind, reception from them. They grudgingly showed me a place to sleep that was just barely adequate. They didn't even show me where the bathroom was. When I had to answer nature's call the only option I had was to open a window and pee down onto the street.

I can't explain the poor treatment I received from these relatives; maybe they were afraid I had lice. It was difficult for me to understand how they could be so cold to me. Before the war food was scarce in Budapest and we would send them provisions from our farm. Now that I needed help from them, they acted as if I was a complete stranger, not the son of family members who helped them when they needed it. My great-uncle and his wife must have survived owing to their connection to their highly placed connections. Or perhaps they had survived in one of the ghettos that Jews were forced into.

I stayed with them for two days until my uncle Dennis arrived to pick me up and take me back to Szolnok to live with him. We got back to Szolnok just before Christmas, 1945. Since I had been taken from school before I could finish the fifth grade, Dennis hired his former professor from the university to tutor me. The tutor helped me to finish grade five, and the sixth grade as well.

My Uncle Dennis was my grandfather's son from a second marriage – grandfather's first wife, my mother's mother, had died. Dennis was about fifteen years younger than my mother and about eight years older than me. Like everyone else in my mother's family, he was very talented musically. When I was about nine years old and Dennis was seventeen, he came to live with us in Szikszó (as I recounted in my first chapter) because my grandfather had thrown him out of the house for playing jazz. Grandfather caught him playing "In the Mood." My grandfather believed that only bums played jazz, but I looked up to Dennis as a very cool guy.

He managed to survive the war by being kept in jail for not wearing the yellow star that all Jews had to wear. He was arrested and put in jail, and he made certain he stayed there by bribing the guards so as not to be deported to Auschwitz or shot. He was not only a cool guy but also a clever one.

Dennis must have known the fate of my parents and my sister, but whenever I asked him about them he would give me only the vaguest of answers. So I still lived in hope that I would soon be reunited with them again.

Dennis's girlfriend, Terri, who was not Jewish, lived with us in Szolnok. She came from a farm close to the city and once every week I had to bicycle out to the farm she came from to pick up provisions for the household.

Dennis owned a dance studio in Szolnok. During the day he gave dance lessons but at night, when I worked there, the studio became a sort of club. People would come to meet and dance. It was very popular; there were always a lot of people and they all smoked, which made the place smelly and smoky. In the days that followed the end of the war I guess that people just wanted to have a good time – and Dennis was more than happy to provide a place for people to do just that. I worked in the coat-check room and helped out generally as best I could.

From mid-winter when I arrived back in Szolnok until the beginning of September 1946, this was my life. I studied, I went to the farm, and I helped out at the dance studio. All this changed in September 1946. One day, Dennis simply disappeared, leaving me alone with Terri. I had no idea why he had gone so abruptly. Terri claimed that he had told her he was afraid he would be drafted into the Hungarian army. It was many years before I discovered what had became of Dennis after his abrupt and mysterious disappearance. At the time I wondered if I would ever see him again.

Terri and I decided that we should to move to Szikszó. I wanted to be with my family in my hometown. My cousin Nandy Morgenstern, who at twenty-five years old was twelve years older than me, had survived the war in one of the worker brigades. He took care of the cousins who survived the *Shoah*. I got word to him that we were coming to Szikszó and that I wanted to try to get my house back. As far as I was concerned the house had been stolen from my family when we were taken away. Nandy helped me in this regard but he was only partially successful. He was only able to arrange for me to get part of the house back. Terri and I had to share it with the people who had taken it from my parents. By this time I realized that only five of my first cousins from my extended family of over fifty people had survived the war. Four of them, including my cousin Tibor, were living with my cousin Nandy in his parents' house.

Nandy was the person who had the sad task of informing me that my parents and my sister had perished at the hands of the Nazis. This for me was the saddest, most devastating moment of my life. I finally had to face the terrible fact that I was alone in the world. Yes, I had some surviving first and second cousins, but they couldn't take the place of the family I had lost. My feelings of desolation were overpowering.

Along with the feelings of anguish I also developed feelings of anger, feelings that stayed with me for many, many years. I remembered well my father saying about those who imprisoned us, "We'll get those bastards." It broke my heart that we wouldn't be able to accomplish this, and that I would have to face the future without my parents and sister. A broken heart is fallow ground in which animosity and choler can grow, and these feelings grew within me. If "*we* couldn't get those bastards," then I would do my utmost to make certain that "those bastards" would never get me and mine.

Anger and sorrow can be a dangerous combination. As I look back over the last eighty-plus years at the life I lived, the decisions I made, the actions I took, I understand now that perhaps it was the combination of sorrow and anger that motivated me to take the reckless chances I took. Perhaps I didn't carefully weigh the consequences of all of my actions because I didn't care about them.

Most, if not all, the survivors of the camps are fearless. There is nothing that could be worse than what we went through at Auschwitz or the other Nazi camps. The feeling that helped me survive my incarceration – the belief that if that other fellow could survive then so could I – also grew in me in the months and years following my return home.

It took me many, many years, probably the better part of my life, to bring these three feelings – sorrow, anger, and fearlessness – into some kind of harmony. As a teenager and a young man I struggled to cope with these emotions. As a grief-stricken and volatile adolescent I felt I had no choice but to try to build some sort of life for myself.

The part of the house that Terri and I arranged to occupy included my parents' bedroom. There was only one bed and we shared it. I was an adolescent only fourteen years old at that time, anxious for my first sexual experience, and I made every effort to have it with Terri. However, she would not oblige. This, as you can understand, caused me great frustration.

When I returned to Szikszó, my old friend Jeno, who used to live next door to us, was still there and we saw each other from time to time. When Jeno and I were friends before the war we were the same age and the same size. When I came back he had grown considerably but I had not, owing to the fact that I was malnourished. Also, Jeno had a girlfriend and I was jealous of him for that. This made me redouble my efforts with Terri, but to no avail.

When Jeno and I resumed our friendship, we got up to some mischievous exploits that could have killed us. The area in and around Szikszó was a battleground for Russian and German troops and after the war there was a large amount of unexploded materiel lying around. Of special interest to Jeno and me was the bazooka ammunition we found. From somewhere in our adolescent brains we got the idea that it would be a good idea to open the bazooka shell, remove the explosive powder, make a large zig-zag design with it, and then light it on fire. We set these fires at night in order to make a strong visual impact. We figured this would at the very least confuse the townspeople and likely scare them, as they would not know how the zig-zag fire came to be.

Jeno was very interested in science and engineering, and he had formed the opinion that if we hammered at the sides of the ammunition, avoiding the ends, we would be able to remove the explosive with no harm to ourselves. We didn't have hammers so we used heavy rocks to open the bazooka ammunition, remove the gunpowder, and make our design. I don't remember how the townspeople reacted to our prank but it was nothing short of amazing that we didn't kill ourselves. A farmer in the area drove his tractor over an unexploded shell and blew himself up.

While I was in Szikszó I tried my hand at being in business. My cousin Nandy found the tractor that my family had owned before the war and he was able to reclaim it without difficulty. We met a man who owned a harvesting machine and we formed a partnership with him, going from farm to farm to work on the harvest. A farmer would bring us his crop and the machines would extract the grain. We charged the farmer 10 percent of the value of the grain. But the Communist government took a dim view of my entrepreneurial efforts and accused my partner and me of committing fraud.

I was brought before a judge on a charge of not paying taxes on our profit. I claimed not to have known anything about this, as my partner was the one who handled all the financial transactions. I pointed out that I was only fourteen years old and so deferred to my older partner in business matters. I felt that this was a very important point – not to mention that harvest was a time of celebration and that, being drunk most of the time, I couldn't be expected to concern myself with taxes. The government official told me that he would get back to me. I understood his message to mean that it would be a good idea to get rid of the tractor and find a way to get out of the country. All the members of my family and our close friends who survived the Holocaust had the desire and the ambition to get out of Hungary. We found Communism to be inhospitable and we could see that anti-Semitism was showing signs of recurring.

This was my introduction to business and I learned two valuable lessons. The first was not to drink while operating heavy equipment. I was drunk so often when working on the tractor and the harvester that I could easily have been killed. The second lesson was that I had mechanical skills. When there was a problem with the machinery I worked with my partner to repair them, and I developed an understanding of mechanical problems with ease. The discovery that I had this ability made it clear to me that whatever I did in the future, if I had the opportunity to develop this skill, it would be a big help.

My dear Rothschild Bácsi had also made his way back to Szikszó and I was delighted to have him as a part of my life again. Dennis had disappeared and Nandy left for Israel soon afterward with my other cousins. Uncle Rothschild was my sole connection to my previous life; without him I would have been completely alone.

He arranged for me to get a job working in a garage in Miskolc. The plan was that I would become a car mechanic. I've always enjoyed working with my hands but I can't say that I enjoyed that job very much as I had to travel by train every day to get to it. I would have much preferred a job closer to home.

Mr Rothschild also took care of the money I received for the sale of the tractor. He thought the best way to handle it was to invest it in wine. He understood that wine got better with age and would therefore increase in value. He was able to procure the wine. But only later when I was in Canada did I find out that the government had confiscated it. The fact that my first couple of attempts at business didn't prove to be successful was due more to the political climate in Hungary after the war, which was hostile to capitalism, than to any shortcoming in my abilities. It was 1946 and I was only fourteen years old, so I was certain I would have other opportunities to exercise my entrepreneurial skills.

At some point Mr Rothschild got wind of the fact that Terri and I were sharing a bed and he didn't think this was a good idea. He also thought there was no future for me in Szikszó and probably not in Hungary at all. He decided it would be best for me to be placed in an orphanage in Budapest. He took me to the Mikéfe Orphanage, where I could learn a trade. The Mikéfe Orphanage had been established by the Jewish community a long time before the war to teach orphans a trade and to help them with schooling. After the war it became a Zionist organization with the object of getting the orphaned youth of Hungary to Israel. The plan then was that I would learn a trade and then emigrate to Israel.

All in all, because of the accusation of fraud and because I felt that there was no future for me in Hungary, I wanted to get out. I also feared that I would be called back to court and I had no idea what fate awaited me if that happened. So I agreed to travel to Budapest with Mr Rothschild and be placed in the orphanage.

Terri left to visit with her family on their farm and Mr Rothschild took me to Budapest while she was gone. When she returned
to Szikszó, my cousin Nandy told her what had transpired and she
returned to her family farm. I never heard from her again.

In preparation for my journey to what would be my new home
in the newly established state of Israel, I took Hebrew lessons at
the orphanage, and on weekends we would go to the Buda hills
and get combat training so that we could join the war against the
British and the Arabs. This was in 1947 and I was fifteen years old.

When it came to choosing a trade, I chose tool making. I had
always been good at working with my hands and I thought that
tool making would be a useful skill in the future. While waiting
for clearance to go to Palestine, I worked in a small shop as an
apprentice toolmaker to learn that trade. All of the kids from the
orphanage, most of whom, like me, were under eighteen, had
already left for France on their way to Palestine. They were awaiting a ship in the port city of Marseilles. However, due to the fact
that the British blockade of Palestine was still in force, they were
unable to continue their journey. This meant that I wouldn't be
able to leave the orphanage to go to Israel.

Rothschild Bácsi, my guardian angel with whom I was in constant contact, came to see me at the orphanage with another
proposition. He suggested that I go to Canada. He told me he had
a contact in Canada who would be able to help me. His contact
was a Mr Toth, whose wife was in Hungary. Uncle Rothschild was
helping Mr Toth's wife by giving her money. He proposed that
when I arrived in Canada I should find her husband, collect the
money and keep it for Uncle Rothschild. He gave me a letter stating that I was his son and authorizing me to collect the money
owed. Unfortunately Mr Rothschild had a very weak understanding of Canadian geography; he had no knowledge of how great
the distances were between cities, and had no idea where Mr Toth
lived. When I got to Canada l looked for Mr Toth – but I never
found him.

For reasons that were never completely clear to me, Mr Rothschild opted to remain in Hungary even as he advised me to leave.
Perhaps he was hopeful that the country would return to the way
it was before the war. Perhaps he felt he was too old to emigrate.

In any event, he had no immediate plans to leave his home country. This was a mistake on his part. After the communists took over, they must have discovered that he knew which of them had been part of the Nazi puppet regime. These men had the ideological flexibility to switch their loyalties from a dictatorship of the right to the dictatorship of the left.

In order to ensure that Mr Rothschild remained silent, at some point after I left Hungary, the government had him arrested and jailed. He remained in prison until the Hungarian uprising of 1956, when he was freed. At that time, he didn't spend any longer in Hungary than he had to and made his way to Israel, the country that he called home for the rest of his life. But he didn't remain in Israel. He immigrated to Canada to join his son, Laci, who by this time had moved to Toronto.

My best friend at the orphanage was Karcsi Rothschild. He had the same family name as Rothschild Bácsi, but was no relation to him. Karcsi's trade was that of an upholsterer and, like me, he thought he would prosper in Canada. We both applied to be a part of the orphan program. Our first application was rejected, not by Canada but because the orphanage cancelled it. I was never certain why the orphanage did that. It seems likely that they hoped to send us to Israel and didn't want us to go to Canada. When Karcsi and I discovered that the orphanage had cancelled our application, we made a second attempt. This time, instead of using the address of the orphanage, we used the address of Karcsi's aunt. The orphanage didn't know about the second application and so could not abort it.

Canada had agreed to take a certain number of orphans who were under the age of eighteen and were healthy. Because of this restriction, Karcsi was unable to take part in the program but I was accepted. I went to the Canadian Consulate in Budapest and was examined by a Canadian doctor. He found me to be healthy and I was sent, along with about thirty other orphans, by train from Budapest to Paris on the first leg of our journey to Canada.

On the train to Paris I met Nick Sebastian and we became very close friends. There were also some young girls on the same train. The girls had food with them and neither Nick nor I had had the forethought to bring any with us. But with a combination of

charm and flirtation we were able to convince the girls to share
their food with us.

When we got to Paris we were placed in a home on the outskirts
of the city for about a month awaiting an opportunity to board a
ship for Canada. The expense of our stay in Paris as well as all the
costs for our trip to Canada were covered by the Jewish Immigrant
Aid Society. The ship we were assigned to was embarking from
Marseilles and we took a train south to that city. When we got
there we discovered that there wasn't enough room on board for
all of us, and four of us had to wait in Marseilles for the next ship.
That first group of young people went to Toronto.

We were told that we would have to wait for three weeks in Marseilles for the next ship. Even though I was in a strange city where
I did not, at that time, speak the language, I was not worried in any
way. I had been through so much that there was very little that
would scare me. I knew the future would be very much better than
the past.

Because we were stranded in Marseilles for two or three weeks,
we were given food coupons by the agency responsible for getting
us to Canada. The food coupons were for meals at a place that was
really nothing more than a soup kitchen. There were a lot of Arabs
in Marseilles, and Nick sold them some of our food coupons. The
coupons he sold them were out of date so we had to hide from
them. Despite our overall fearlessness, we *were* afraid these Arabs
would kill us if they found us.

Nick's larcenous exploits were an unfortunate part of his character. Many years later I had occasion to have to deal with this
aspect of his personality. But in Marseilles I thought that Nick, like
me, was simply a risk taker. I enjoyed his company because he was
very funny and had a wonderful sense of derring-do.

Beyond that, our wait in Marseilles was not very exciting. There
were very nice beaches in that part of France, and the four of us
spent some of our time beachcombing. But mostly we spent our
time contemplating what life would be like in Canada. We knew
very little about Canada at that time. We had heard that there were
lots of lakes and forests, and that it was the country where the
Dionne quintuplets were born. We wondered whether we would
end up in a forest or a city. But we knew it was a big country with

only fourteen million people, so we were certain that we would find opportunities there to make something of ourselves in a new life.

Our only immediate concern was whether there would be sufficient food on the ship. We had no idea how an ocean-going ship operated so, to ensure that we would have enough to eat, we arranged to get food for our voyage. This time we were over-prepared; we were the only four passengers to board the ship with our own food.

* * *

I referred earlier to the fact that my Uncle Dennis, with whom I had been living in Szolnok, disappeared one day leaving me with his girlfriend, Terri. In a way this event was the indirect reason I immigrated to Canada. If Uncle Rothschild had not been concerned about my living with and sharing a bed with Terri, he might not have placed me in the orphanage, and if I had not been in the orphanage during the final days of the British blockade of Israel, he might not have suggested that I set sail for Canada. So, in a way, I have Uncle Dennis's disappearance to thank for all the good things that happened to me as a result of it. But I never stopped wondering what became of my Uncle Dennis and why he ran off without so much as a note of explanation.

In 1952 or 1953 immigrants were continuing to arrive in Canada. One of the families that immigrated to Montreal was a Hungarian family named Kraus who had come to Canada from Holland. I met and became friendly with Mr Kraus and, like all survivors of the Holocaust, we traded stories. Mr Kraus was held in a slave labour camp and after the war he went to Holland because he had some good friends there. In the course of our conversations he told me about a friend of his named Dennis Komaromi. In surprise, I told him that Dennis was my long-lost uncle.

It turned out that Dennis had been living in Amsterdam working for the Remington Company repairing typewriters. I got his address from Mr Kraus and began a correspondence with my Uncle Dennis that continued for years.

Dennis had developed tuberculosis and he was a patient in a sanatorium. By 1953 I had a bit of money so I was able to help him.

When Dennis had recovered from his sickness he left the sanatorium and sent me a photograph of himself with his new car. I couldn't afford a car because I was sending whatever spare money I had to Uncle Dennis – and he used it to buy a car! Again he disappointed me.

Dennis had some relatives on his mother's side in Youngstown, Ohio, and he was able to immigrate to the United States where he continued to work for the Remington Rand Company repairing typewriters. We had many opportunities to meet after he moved to Youngstown and just about every time I saw him I tried to get him to tell me why he had left me and Terri so abruptly. But he never wanted to talk to me about the past. He wouldn't even look me in the eye when I broached the subject. He was kind to my children, though. Whenever he visited he brought gifts for them and he got along very well with my wife, Eleanor.

Eventually he met and married a divorcee in Cleveland. He became a stepfather to the woman's two sons and began working for his father-in-law. His father-in-law had a small business making sausages that they sold to small shops in and around Cleveland. Dennis ended up a sausage maker. He took over the business from his father-in-law.

It was not long after this that his tuberculosis returned and he developed cancer as well. We heard from his wife that he was very sick and so I went to visit him. He expressed regret for the way he had treated me and told me that if we had stayed together his life would have been much different because I always succeeded at whatever I did. He died a few days later, just in his early fifties. All in all, he seemed to have had a pretty tough life after leaving Hungary.

Even on his deathbed he chose not to explain his behaviour from all those years ago. I thought that he would have wanted to die with a clear conscience. But apparently Uncle Dennis had no such desire. I loved him just the same, and appreciated all that he had done for me when I returned home from Auschwitz, but just as I don't know why he disappeared, I don't understand why he refused to tell me.

# 4

# Hungary for Canada

I came to Canada as a part of what is known as the War Orphans Project. At the time I immigrated my principal contact was with the Jewish Immigrant Aid Society (JIAS). I very much appreciated all that this wonderful organization did to make my journey to Canada possible and for their help in getting me settled in my new country. At the time, though, I was unaware of all the other people who worked so hard to make the Orphans Project work. It was only after my writing partner, Richard King, did some archival research that I discovered the people and the organizations that were behind the success of the Orphans Project. It is entirely possible that I would not have been able to come to Canada had it not been for their efforts.

Following the First World War, Canada's immigration policy was frankly anti-Semitic. The government's stated policy was to prevent the immigration of people who were of "races that cannot be assimilated without social or economic loss to Canada."* As if that wasn't clear enough, the government stipulated that it wanted people who were similar in "'racial characteristics' to the Anglo-Canadian majority."† Put bluntly: Jews were not welcome.

Following the Second World War, in 1947, a delegation from the Canadian Jewish Congress was able to convince the government of Canada to establish the War Orphans Project, which allowed for

* Quoted in Irving Abella and Harold Troper, *None Is Too Many: Canada and the Jews of Europe, 1933–1948* (Toronto: University of Toronto Press, 2012), xii.
† Ibid.

over a thousand Jewish children under the age of eighteen to enter Canada. This project was actually the re-establishment of a program that had been set up in 1942 to rescue Jewish orphans from Vichy, France. The 1942 program was never actually put into effect. The Nazi occupation of France put an end to the project before it could bring a single orphan from France to Canada.*

The Canadian Jewish Congress sent Dr Manfred Saalheimer to Europe to locate a thousand Jewish orphans eligible for immigration to Canada. Dr Saalheimer was a German-Jewish lawyer who had escaped from Germany to England at the outbreak of the war. The British had rounded him up along with a group of 2,290 Germans they considered to be enemy aliens, to be interned in Farnham, Quebec.† Following the war Dr Saalheimer opted to remain in Canada and he worked on the War Orphans Project for the Canadian Jewish Congress.

It was agreed that the paperwork for the Jewish orphans would be handled in Paris and that is why, once I was accepted for immigration to Canada, I was taken to that city.

My paperwork was completed at some point during this process and it is interesting to look back at it and see how accurately the person who filled out the form was able to describe me in five short sentences. The form describes me as tall and of medium weight and goes on to say: "At school he was a good student, he was deported when he was 12 years old. At present he is apprenticed as a metal turner. He does not know yet whether he wishes to continue his trade overseas. He likes reading and has many friends. He is fond of sports, especially football."

And so I began my journey to Canada.

Early in September of 1948 my friend Nick Sebastian and I and the two other young people who didn't make it onto the previous ship boarded the MS *Sobieski*, an 11,000-ton Polish-registered ship. The ship was a luxury liner, but we were housed in the hold near the engine room, with the staff. It was a very rough crossing in that we hit a terrible storm that kept us stationary for three days. It

---

* The information regarding the War Orphans Project comes from: Fraidie Martz, *Open Your Hearts: The Story of the Jewish War Orphans in Canada* (Montreal: Véhicule Press, 1966).

† Ibid., 83.

caused a large number of people on board to get very sick. The storm had very little effect on Nick or me, though; neither of us got sick.

It didn't take long for Nick and me to learn that it hadn't been necessary to bring food on board with us. We ate with the crew in the kitchen – and there was lots of food. From my perspective – the perspective of someone who knew too well what it was like to live on the verge of starvation – it was a delight to have so much available to eat. I have to admit that it did seem to me that there was too much food. But then again, everything was a learning experience for me.

The biggest problem we had on the ship was language. The crew was Polish, and I had only a rudimentary knowledge of that language – the few words and phrases I had picked up at Auschwitz. I was unable to carry on a conversation. Because the ship sailed from Marseilles there were French-speaking people aboard, but I didn't speak French. And no one on the ship, other than the young immigrants who were travelling with me, spoke Yiddish. There were other immigrants on the ship, families with young children, but we didn't have much to do with them.

We only saw the crew at meal times and at night. We were housed in a large room with about thirty beds arranged in tiers three high. There was very little to do and we passed the time by playing cards.

In order to break up the boredom of life on the ship, Nick and I would sneak up to the areas where the better classes of guests spent their time. Every time we tried this, we were caught and chased out of the upper decks, but we never gave up. It was fun and it was something to do. And, really, when we were caught by the staff there was very little they could do to us. They couldn't throw us overboard; they could only chase us back down to the hold until we tried to get to the upper decks again.

We finally arrived in the port of Halifax on Sunday, 19 September 1948. I had a small box with all my worldly possessions in it, but when I saw Halifax from the ship I made the decision to start my new life in Canada with nothing from my old life in Europe. I threw my belongings overboard and arrived with nothing in my pockets but my hands.

Joseph Kage, who immigrated to Canada with his family from the city of Minsk when he was five years old, was in 1948 the director of social services for the Jewish Immigrant Aid Society.* Before this he had been a professor at the McGill University School of Social Work. He and his staff created the programs that provided counselling and helped immigrant orphans settle in Canada and integrate into their new country. These programs were designed to provide us with living accommodations, and with jobs or educational opportunities for those who desired them.† My first contact with the JIAS was in Halifax. A couple of women from the society were on the docks to meet us. As a first step in acclimatizing us to our new country, we were taken to the home of a Jewish family. They spoke Yiddish and we had a very nice visit with them. That evening they put us on the train to Montreal.

We arrived in Montreal two days later, on 21 September. Someone from the JIAS met us at the train station and took us to a sort of Welcome Centre where we lived for about two weeks. It was located on Jeanne Mance Street between Villeneuve and Mount Royal, very close to the YMHA, the Davis Y building. From the moment we arrived we were treated with kindness and respect. A JIAS social worker worked with me to help me get settled. I was offered the choice of going to school or getting a job. I requested a job where there was food; I was determined never to risk being hungry again! The social worker got me a job in a bakery, Richstone Bakery, which was located on St Lawrence Boulevard near the corner of Rachel. I worked the night shift there and was able to stuff myself with as much bread and cake as I wanted. My friend Nick also got a job there.

The JIAS also took care of our living situation in that they found a family who provided room and board. Nick and I lived with a family by the name of Sanfer, and we shared a room. Their apart-

---

* The biographical information concerning Joseph Kage comes from two obituaries. One is from the *Globe and Mail* written by Ron Csillag and published on 29 October 1996 in the "Lives Lived" section of the newspaper. The other one comes from an unnamed source that I believe to be *The Gazette*.

† Joseph Kage, *With Faith and Thanksgiving* (Montreal: Eagle Publishing Co. Limited, 1962), 125–9 and following; Martz, *Open Your Hearts*.

ment was on St Lawrence very close to where we worked. The Sanfers were a very nice family, originally from Winnipeg. They later moved back there.

I arrived in Canada with only the clothes on my back, and this was true for most of the others who arrived with me. The JIAS social worker arranged for us to go to the Schreter clothing store on St Lawrence to get new clothes. Joe Schreter, himself an immigrant from Hungary who had been in Montreal for many years, outfitted me and the others with everything we needed. He didn't ask us for any money. His only request was that, when we were on our feet and could afford to buy clothing, we shop at the Schreter store. I was pleased to be able to shop there for about fifty years in order to show my gratitude to a family that went out of its way to make me feel welcome in my new country.

My experience with the Schreter family was the first example I had, other than that of my father and Rothschild Bácsi, of someone giving for the sake of doing good without the expectation of getting something in return. Joe Schreter said that giving was its own satisfaction. His lesson, which in my mind echoed my father's belief that it was important to give a little more to make people feel good, stayed with me for the rest of my life. Joe Schreter replanted the seed of giving for the sake of giving that had first been planted in me by my father and Mr Rothschild.

Another benefit that the JIAS provided was a free year's membership at the YMHA, the Davis Y. I always liked sports and working out, and I took advantage of the membership to further my interest in physical fitness. In Hungary I played soccer as often as I could. I joined a team in Montreal but I didn't like the other players because I didn't think they were doing their best. In sports, in fact in every endeavour, it is important to me to always do my best.

Nick had been a wrestler in Hungary and he took up the sport again in Montreal. It was through Nick that I became acquainted with wrestling and I grew to love the sport. The people I met in the wrestling program at the Y during the year of my free membership were very nice; they welcomed me in the sport and also welcomed me to their homes. What I liked and continue to like about wrestling is that it is an individual sport that tests both physical skill and strategy. The two wrestling coaches I trained with at the Y, Harry Hirschenkoff and Harry Joffe, were more than kind to me. They trained me as best they could and acted in some ways like surrogate fathers. The coaches invited me into their homes and took me on fishing trips.

Two other aspects of wrestling appealed to me. The sport allowed me to prove to myself that I could stand up to anybody. In Szikszó when we were chased by anti-Semites we ran away. I would never run away again. Wrestling helped me to deal with the anger I felt for what my family and I had been through in Europe. I also felt that the Jews in Europe were seen as sissies by the Gentiles, and that is partly why they felt they could make scapegoats out of us – blame us for all their problems. As a wrestler I was demonstrating that I was not a sissy and that I would not run away from a fight.

* * *

In addition to my salary, I had access to a subsidy from the JIAS. I earned $15 a week at my job at the bakery (the equivalent of roughly $150 in 2017 dollars). The JIAS calculated that I needed $25 a week to live on (roughly $250 today) and they would give me the extra $10 if I could make a budget showing that I needed it. I did my best to create a budget to cover that amount but I couldn't bring my expenses up to $25 a week. Twenty-two dollars was as much as I could honestly claim I needed to live on. I even entered shaving cream and razor blades as expenses despite the fact that at sixteen I was still too young to shave!

After we had been at the Richstone Bakery for a while, Nick and I changed jobs and found employment with a company that manufactured buttons for the fur industry. The buttons were made of small balls of *papier mâché* that were covered with fur and were used for fur coats. My salary at that job was $25 a week, which meant that I didn't have to make a budget for the JIAS in order to get extra money. This gave me a feeling of independence as I was earning the money I needed to live on.

Nick and I didn't stay with the button manufacturer for very long. I didn't like the job at all. The atmosphere was very regimented. Our boss, a German Jew, was constantly checking our work and demanding that we work faster. On the other hand, I admit that we weren't the best employees in the company. On the ground floor of the building where we worked there was a restaurant with a pinball machine. Nick and I had a ten-minute break during which we played pinball. Neither of us had ever seen a pinball machine before we came to Montreal, and we enjoyed the novelty of the game, the flashing lights and loud pinging noises that occurred whenever we scored points. As it turned out, we were quite good at the game and racked up a lot of free games, the reward for winning at pinball. Because we had to get back to work in ten minutes, we usually sacrificed the free games. But at one point, when we didn't care whether or not we lost our jobs, we played all our free games and returned to work after an hour or more. Of course we were fired.

Our next job was with a man called Mr Kaufman. He had a business trading in used boxes and jute bags. We would drive around in a truck with Mr Kaufman at the wheel and pick up boxes and bags from outside the Steinberg's (a now defunct grocery chain) warehouse where the workers discarded them. We would then sell them back to the farmers, who used them to ship their produce to Steinberg's and other grocery stores. We would also go to the Canadian Pacific Railway yards, where we picked up jute bags that the company put in the garbage. We cleaned the bags up as best we could and straightened them out before we sold them to the farmers. We each earned sixty-five cents an hour at this job. We started working for Mr Kaufman in December, and as the weather got colder the work became miserable. We were unprepared for the cold of the Canadian winter, and riding in the back of the truck gave us a rough introduction to it. We soon decided to get work where we could work indoors.

For the first time, we looked for jobs separately because we felt more confident in our ability to communicate in English. We were adjusting to life in Canada and felt independent, that each of us could manage on our own.

I got a job as a cutter in a sportswear factory at St Dominique and Rachel. At the time this was at the heart of the needle trade in Montreal. I stayed at that job until I heard that good money could be earned working on a tobacco farm in Ontario. I borrowed some money for the trip to the tobacco region from Nick (he was better at saving money than I was). At that time I had the bad habit of spending everything I had.

In June of 1949 I made my way to the town of Delhi in western Ontario, the heart of the "tobacco belt" in Canada. There was no formal hiring procedure in place. In order to get a job you had to walk up and down the main street hoping to be noticed by one of the farmers. They sat in their trucks and would call you over if they thought you would be a good tobacco picker. It took longer to find a job than I anticipated, so I had to spend my first few nights in Delhi at a hostel of sorts at a cost of fifty cents a night. Finally, I was hired by a Hungarian farmer. This was a stroke of good luck as we spoke the same language. I was paid $11.00 a day plus room and board.

The money was excellent but the work was very hard. To harvest tobacco I learned to bend down, grab the tobacco plant from the bottom and break it from its stem. I had to hold the leaves under my arm. A horse and sled would ride through the fields and we'd put the tobacco into the dray. The tobacco was then taken to a drying area where women tied it to sticks for drying. There were six men and six women working on this tobacco farm. We worked six days a week during the harvest, which lasted six weeks. Most of the workers were Aboriginal people. They were very experienced at harvesting tobacco and, better yet, they were excellent at massaging my aching back. Because I was taller than the other workers I had to bend lower than they did to be able to grab the plant at its base and snap it off at its stem. The best thing about working on a farm, though, was that we had an unlimited amount of food.

My boss's name was Mr Cerenko, and over the time that I worked for him on the harvest he grew to like me. He and his wife had no children and they offered me the opportunity to stay with them, in effect to become a member of their family. However, by that time I had started to develop friendships in Montreal and I had also started to participate in Olympic wrestling. I was unwilling to give this up and move to a small town in Ontario and become a farmer. I told Mr Cerenko that if he wanted to see me again he should take a picture.

Looking back at that period I realize that I was arrogant and aggressive at that time. I attribute this to the fact that as a result of my experiences in Auschwitz I was determined to be a dominant character in any situation. I think I took this feeling a little too far with Mr Cerenko. After all he *was* offering to help me.

After the harvest I went to Toronto to see friends of mine who had been on the first ship to have left the port of Marseilles. I had a good time with them, and by the time I got back to Montreal I had spent most of the money I had earned harvesting tobacco. But I made sure that I saved enough that I could pay Nick back the money I had borrowed from him.

Throughout this time I never forgot Karcsi, my best friend at the orphanage in Budapest. He was older than I was and he became a big brother to me, and my protector. He was a very strong young man and when I got into fights at the orphanage he would come to my defence. Because he was eighteen, two years older than me, he was not accepted to be part of the orphan project organized by the Canadian government to bring orphans to Canada, as the participants had to be under that age. Karcsi believed that his trade as an upholsterer was valuable and he had a good job in Budapest. He was sure he would have very little difficulty in establishing his own upholstery shop anywhere other than Hungary. Karcsi wanted to immigrate to Canada because that is where I was headed. His other option was to immigrate to the United States where he had some relatives.

My aim was to get a job in an upholstering factory so that, after proving myself as a good employee, I could ask my boss to sponsor Karcsi. If my plan worked he would be able to come to Canada to join me.

Soon after I got back to Montreal after working on the tobacco harvest I began my search for a job in upholstery. My English was now good enough to search the classified section of the *Montreal Star* and I saw an ad for a job at an upholstering company called Montreal Upholstering. I applied for the job and was lucky enough to get it. I wrote to tell Karcsi of my good fortune and told him I would broach the subject of sponsoring him after I had been on the job for a while. I wanted Karcsi to come to Canada because we were very close friends.

My boss at Montreal Upholstering was a man named Max Friedman who, with his brother Ben, owned the factory. At the time, the Friedman brothers were getting ready to retire and they brought their sons into the business with the idea that they would take it over. Max's son Sydney was in charge of sales and Ben's son Leonard handled the administration and managed the factory. I worked with Max at the cutting table for about a year until he retired, at which point I took charge of the cutting department.

By the time I felt confident enough to ask Max Friedman to sponsor Karcsi so that he could join me in Canada, I had lost contact with my friend. He had disappeared. My letters to him went unanswered. In the last letter I had from him he had told me he was in Vienna and was planning to go to Paris. He had some relatives in the United States and hoped to be able to get papers to join them. He heard that it would be difficult to get immigration documents from Austria so he thought he would try his luck from France. And that was the last I heard from him. I never got the chance to tell him that I had a job for him in the upholstery business and that I wanted to try to get him sponsored so he could join me in Montreal.

Over the years that followed, a period during which I started my own business, got married, and started to raise a family, I thought often about Karcsi and wondered what had become of him, what could explain his sudden disappearance. I heard nothing from him until much later, when he turned up again in a surprising way.

One day in 1964, some fifteen years after my last letter from Karcsi, my wife, Eleanor, received a phone call from the Canadian Red Cross. The person who called told her that someone by the name of Andy Adler was looking for a person by the name of George Reinitz. Eleanor took a phone number from the caller and when I called back I learned that the person who was looking for me had previously had the name Rothschild and he was now living in Australia. I realized that Karcsi had found me after so many years. The person I spoke to at the Red Cross gave me Karcsi's phone number and I called him in Australia. Finally, Karcsi and I had found one another. He told me the rest of his story – the events that had occurred since the time he was in Vienna.

Karcsi Rothschild changed his name to Andy Adler so that he would be at the head of the list of people eligible to immigrate to Canada or the United States. He decided to put his plan to go to France into effect and he got caught trying to sneak into France from Austria. The Austrian authorities put him in jail.

At that time representatives of the Australian government were looking for immigrants. They went into the jails of Austria looking for white people who were able to work. Andy more than met the criteria. The Australians gave him some papers to sign and, even though he didn't know what he was agreeing to as he didn't know English, he knew that whatever it was would be better than being in jail. He was taken out of jail and sent to Australia. When he got there he was put to work in the jungle building the railway. He had obviously signed some sort of agreement to work on the railroad in exchange for immigrant status in Australia. After two years of working on the railway he ended up in a small town repairing furniture. He married and made a life for himself in Australia.

I was extremely happy when he was able to visit Canada to renew our friendship and meet my family. Even after such a long absence my feelings for Karcsi had not changed. The emotion that was part of my original wish to bring him to Canada so that we could work together never left me.

In 2001 I received an email from Karcsi telling me that he had been diagnosed with cancer and had only a short time to live. He wanted very much to be able to say goodbye to me and I had the same strong desire to see him one more time. Even though we had lost contact with one another for a long period of time, we never forgot one another. I always thought of him more as a brother than a friend. Eleanor and I made the journey to Australia to see Karcsi one last time.

At the end of our visit, when we had to say goodbye, Karcsi and I were both overcome with emotion. We had come into each other's lives as a result of one of the worst periods in human history and we had survived. At a point where we had no one else we had each other. This made leaving him again for the final time a deeply upsetting moment. Saying good-bye to a loved one doesn't get easier with repetition. In fact it gets harder, as it brings to mind all the other times when I have had to part with those I cared for. Karcsi has a place in my heart and I think of him often.

\* \* \*

When I left Montreal to work on the tobacco farm, it was with the understanding that my friend Nick and I would continue to live together on my return. But when I got back from the farm I was surprised and disappointed to discover that Nick had moved out of the house where we boarded together, and was living somewhere else with other friends. He didn't consider me in his plans; he clearly gave little thought to the fact that I would need a place to live when I returned from Ontario. Loyalty is a very strong emotion for me and I clearly felt more loyalty toward Nick than he did to me. But I got over my disappointment, and Nick and I remained friends and even went into business together. Looking back over events, though, I think I probably should have taken this as an insight into Nick's character, but I was young and forgiving so I set about finding another place to live. I learned many years later that my intuition about Nick's character had been correct.

I found a place with another friend, a room-and-board rental on St Urbain, not far from my job at Montreal Upholstering. I was now making enough money to be able to treat myself to a few luxuries. I was able to go to nightclubs and go on dates, and Nick and I bought a car together – a 1947 Mercury, On weekends we drove to the Laurentian Mountains north of Montreal and went fishing. We also made good use of the car when we had dates.

At the Y I met a fellow named Zoltan Prauner. Like me, he had immigrated to Canada from Hungary. He was not one of my wrestling friends; he was more interested in gymnastics and body-building. He lived with Sam and Annie Pugatch, a married couple, on what was then Maplewood Avenue (the street is now called Edouard Monpetit). They had no children of their own, and they treated Zoltan like a son.

Annie and Sam Pugatch were originally from Russia. They were well educated; Annie had graduated with a degree in Russian Literature from the university in St Petersburg. They were Communists but, because they were Trotskyites, they had to get out of the country after Stalin came to power. Auntie Annie, as I came to call her, was a brave and adventurous woman. She told us she had been in a beer hall in Munich where Hitler held his rallies. If the crowd had discovered that she was Jewish they would have lynched her on the spot.

She had a brother, Abe Levine, who lived in New York and she flew down to visit him at a time when very few people travelled on airplanes. He was very successful and wanted to help her out financially, but she refused. Abe wanted Annie to immigrate to the United States but this would have been impossible for her. Because of her membership in the Communist Party in Russia, Annie would not have been accepted as an immigrant to the United States. In any event she wanted to have the satisfaction of being self-sufficient and preferred to stay in Canada.

After Zoltan had been living with Annie and Sam for a while a very sad event occurred: Sam committed suicide. I never knew why he took this ultimate step other than the fact that had been depressed for a long time, probably suffering from what was called *mal du siècle*. Over time I became more and more friendly with Zoltan and he occasionally invited me to his place for dinner. He introduced me to Annie. She was a warm and welcoming person and we became instant friends. She insisted that I call her Auntie Annie.

When Auntie Annie recovered from her grief, she very generously offered to move into the den, the room Zoltan was occupying, so that he and I could share the larger bedroom that she had occupied with Sam. Having an extra boarder would give her some additional income. From my perspective this was a very lucky break. Auntie Annie became a second mother to me, and one of the most important influences in my life.

At some point in the early fifties Annie's brother Abe was able to convince her to come to New York to live with him and his wife on a temporary basis, as she would not likely have been able to get a green card due to her radical background. She tried this for six months or so but returned to Montreal when she felt that her brother was paying more attention to her than to his wife. She believed her presence would cause family problems that would ultimately damage her relationship with Abe and his wife and she didn't want to be put in that position. I also think that she missed her life in Montreal with Zoltan and me – her surrogate sons.

While I lived with Auntie Annie we would have discussions on all sorts of subjects, from history to politics to art. Not only was Auntie well educated she was also well read. My conversations with her were like a university education for me. I had only been able to complete the sixth grade in Hungary and at the orphanage I focused on learning a trade, so I was fortunate to be living with someone who could help me satisfy my thirst for knowledge. For example, Annie was interested in the French Revolution for a time, and as she did a lot of reading on the subject it became a topic of conversation for us. Before I lived with her I had no idea there even had been a French Revolution.

Auntie Annie had more than an intellectual interest in history. She had witnessed one of the most important historical events of the twentieth century. She had been a young woman living in Russia when the Revolution broke out and she had seen history unfold. She told us of the famine that gripped St Petersburg while she lived there in 1917. The residents of that city faced starvation as the German army did its best to prevent any food from getting in.

Zoltan had no interest in money or even in a career. When he lived with Auntie Annie and me he had a low-level job in the textile industry examining fabric. He was more interested in art and reading than in material possessions or a lavish lifestyle. He was a very talented artist and spent a lot of his free time drawing. He introduced me to the world of art. He was interested not only in the visual arts but also in the performing arts, especially music and opera. His love of music came from his childhood; his father was involved in some way with the Budapest Opera House. From the time that I lived with Zoltan to the present day I have done my best to enjoy music whenever and wherever I can.

His love of music, which he shared with me, took me back to my childhood and to my mother's love of music and skill at playing the piano. This is my way of honouring my mother's gift of music to me. When I listen to classical music, especially Beethoven and Mozart, I am reminded of how my mother used to say that I took after my father in all ways except for my blue eyes. Even now I have vivid dreams of my mother playing some of her favourite pieces on the piano.

Zoltan and I lived with Auntie Annie from about 1949 until the end of 1953, at which time he got married and moved to Calgary. During the three or four years we spent together, I learned a great deal about the arts from him and Auntie. Thanks to them I have an appreciation for the world of art and music and feel that they bring me, and all those who appreciate them, an inner peace to the soul.

After Zoltan left Montreal I only saw him once, when I was in Calgary for a wrestling tournament. He then worked as a commercial artist and had two grown children. Even though I haven't seen him in years I look back on our days together with great fondness.

Auntie Annie had a very good knowledge of Russian opera, and she and her friends would talk often about opera and listen to *Boris Godunov* and *Faust*. When she was a young woman in St Petersburg she particularly loved the singing of the great Russian baritone Feodor Chaliapin. Annie thought I had a talent for singing and found someone to test my musical ability. The man she found met with me and said of my ability to sing, "I will let you know." I can't have impressed him with my musical ability – I still haven't heard from him.

Overall, I trace my interest in the arts to my mother, Auntie Annie, and Zoltan. It is thanks to them that I am able to derive pleasure and positive feelings from attending concerts and the opera, and visiting art museums.

* * *

In my early days in Montreal I divided my free time between wrestling at the Y and hanging out at the Hungarian Club. These were contradictory activities. At the Y, I spent time with people who wanted to be the best they could in wrestling. It was a positive and encouraging atmosphere.

The Hungarian Club was located on St Lawrence near the corner of Prince Arthur. The club was formed by Hungarians who had come to Canada before the war and it was a place I could hang out and play pool. The old-timers, as we called the founding members, were very helpful to the new arrivals. They taught us what they could about the laws and customs of Canada and they would help some of us find jobs. But I have to admit that the guys I befriended at the Hungarian Club, my poolroom buddies, were not a positive influence on me. They were a rougher crowd than my friends from the Y. They were involved in all sorts of petty crimes such as shoplifting at Birks, an expensive jewelry store in Montreal.

I went with them on some of these escapades but never shoplifted myself or committed any other crime. My job was to stand at the place these guys wanted to shoplift. I am very tall and I wore a big coat in those days so I could provide cover for their larcenous activities. I liked those guys because they were tough and I wanted to show the world how tough I was.

Most of my poolroom companions didn't do all that well in life. Two of them, cousins, thought they had the skill to become boxers. They trained for a fight and were able to get into a scheduled match at the Monument-National theatre. A group of us from the Hungarian Club went to the fight in order to cheer them on. However, these two guys had almost no talent in the ring and were quickly eliminated. Their career as boxers ended before they began. Others of this gang moved to Toronto. They were too well known by the police in Montreal and so could not ply their trade of being petty criminals.

Frank, one of the guys from my poolroom days, turned up about ten years later. By this time Nick and I had opened Jaymar, and Frank somehow tracked me down. He called me and we arranged to meet at my factory to reminisce about old times. He told me that he was divorced with two children. He wanted to borrow money from me in order to make his child support payments. Frank told me an involved and sad story that he expected me to fall for. I had learned enough in my days at the pool hall to know that he, like the other guys we hung out with, were skilled con artists.

When Frank realized that I wouldn't swallow the child support story, he tried another approach. He told me he had a scheme he wanted to start in Toronto that would allow him to pay me back at some indeterminate point in the future. His scheme, which involved forging payroll cheques and cashing them before the banks caught on to the scam, was beyond foolish and was certain to land him in jail again. I usually try to help those who need it but I declined to participate in Frank's crazy endeavour.

While Frank and I were talking, I noticed one of my employees pacing back and forth in front of my office looking at Frank and then looking away. He kept this up for some time until Frank noticed the guy. At this point, they fell into one another's arms like lost brothers, both yelling "Dorchester!" It turned out that they had been inmates together at the Dorchester Penitentiary in New Brunswick and hadn't seen one another since their release. It was nice to witness this reunion but, truthfully, I was even happier when Frank left in a huff because of my refusal to lend him money. I wanted to put my pool-hall days behind me.

As a consequence of my feelings of anger and my sometimes belligerent attitude, I was ready to get into a fight at the slightest provocation. Most of the fights I got into were over very minor issues. If I felt that someone stole a parking spot I had my eye on, it would lead to trading insults and usually ended with the exchange of punches. Looking back on it I realize that my behaviour was not as mature as it should have been. But I also understood that it came from a place deep within me that was determined never to be pushed around again.

There were a couple of times when I thought I had killed the guys I street-fought with. When I was in my early twenties I dated a woman by the name of Frances. She owned a horse and in those days it was possible to rent horses on Mount Royal and we used to go riding together on weekends. One night, after leaving a nightclub near St Lawrence and Ste Catherine, we were walking west on Ste Catherine when three guys approached us. As they passed us one of them bumped into Frances, pushing her into me. I stopped and confronted them by asking, "What the hell are you doing?" They didn't respond, and the guy who had shoved Frances hit me.

I was used to being hit. In wrestling we get hit all the time. And I was certainly not going to back down. Another of the guys grabbed me from behind but I was able to shake him off. I picked up the smallest of the three by grabbing him between the legs with one hand and by the shoulders with the other and threw him on the ground – a wrestling move I quickly adapted to street fighting. The guy on the ground didn't move so now I was fighting two men. The instigator of the fight, seeing that I was not about to back down and would very likely beat him and his friend up, pulled out a gun and claimed he was a cop. Luckily for me, at that exact moment, a car pulled up with another three guys in it and told me to jump in. They had seen the entire series of events, from the first shove to the pulling of the gun, and they saved me. Frances by this time was long gone; she had hailed a cab and headed home.

The guys in the car dropped me off far from the fight and I made my way home. But as I cooled down I began to worry that I had killed the guy I had thrown to the ground. If he had hit his head on the sidewalk with any kind of force he could have died. I didn't remember seeing any blood on the sidewalk but it was dark out and by then I was focused on his two friends. For the next few days I made certain to listen to every radio newscast I could in order to learn if someone had been killed in a street fight on Ste Catherine near St Lawrence. There was no news of a death, so I was satisfied that the three fellows had left the scene bruised but alive.

Several years later, when I was married and Eleanor and I were living in Chomedey, we went out to dinner at a restaurant on Labelle Boulevard. We chose a booth next to the wall of the eatery. There was a bar opposite us where a couple of fellows were drinking and talking in loud voices. One of the guys, probably recognizing that I was Jewish, made an anti-Semitic remark – something to the effect that "they all should have been killed." I got up from the table and confronted the man by saying, "You know I'm Jewish." He replied that we got what we deserved. For some reason I had my keys in my hand and I slapped the fellow across the face with my keys, cutting into his flesh. He bled profusely from the blow. He was too stunned to do anything, but his friend got up from his bar stool and shoved me. I gave him a hard whack with the heel of my hand on his cheekbone close to his ear. At Auschwitz the Ukrainian *kapos* used to hit us that way. It hurts a lot more than a punch with a closed fist and seriously stuns the victim.

While I was trashing these two guys, Eleanor was screaming at me to stop. When I finished with the second fellow, Eleanor and I made a hasty retreat. I was pretty certain that someone would call the cops and I didn't want to have any trouble with them. Needless to say, we never went back to that restaurant.

It was while I was hanging out with the guys from the poolroom that I decided to change the tattoo I had been given at Auschwitz. I got tired of answering questions about it and I wanted to put the past behind me. I had the word "Canada" tattooed over the number in order to honour my new life in my new country.

With time, the positive aspects of my life in wrestling and Auntie Annie's interest in my behaviour pulled me away from the negative influence of the pool room and the crowd that hung out there.

\* \* \*

I was working hard and doing very well at my job at Montreal Upholstering. I worked on the cutting table helping my boss, Max Friedman, one of the two brothers who owned the business, cutting fabric for the furniture we manufactured. When Max retired I was promoted to the head of the cutting department and I hired two people to work under my supervision. The department was running very smoothly and the Friedmans gave me another promotion.

I was put in charge of the upholstering department, where I had a staff of fifteen people and was responsible for the overall quality of the work that went into making furniture. The workers were paid on a piecework basis and I had the responsibility of signing off on each piece of furniture that they made. I worked for Montreal Upholstering for seven years and in that time I made it my business to understand all aspects of furniture production. This included ordering raw materials and meeting with our suppliers and customers.

The first five or six years of my life in Canada were a period of adjustment. I had to learn a new language – two new languages actually – and adapt to a way of life that was completely new to me. I arrived in Canada as a sixteen-year-old who had been through more tough experiences than most people – certainly most Canadians – face in a lifetime.

Canadians had trouble understanding what we had gone through in the war years in Europe. Many of my co-workers would ask questions about my experiences during the war. I did my best to answer them and discovered that they were more curious than sympathetic. One of my fellow workers, Alcide Jonette, who later became a good friend and my first employee when I went into business for myself, told me that things had been very difficult in Quebec as well – that during the war the taverns had to close early! It was a hard lesson to learn; that no one really cared about the events that had so ravaged my entire family. I had to accept that it was pointless to look for sympathy from my Canadian friends and colleagues. I learned that, sadly, you can't expect people to get involved in the misfortunes of others.

I missed my family terribly. The feelings of emptiness never left me. There was a hole in my heart where the love of family used to reside. Annie did her best to fill the void. I arrived in Canada without material possessions but I brought with me a great deal of anger for what had happened to me and those I loved. In my early days in Montreal I had trouble coping with the anger that was very near the surface. There were times when feelings of sadness and anger so overpowered me that I felt like taking a baseball bat and beating the stuffing out of anyone who got in my way.

Over time I was able to exorcise this demon. Wrestling was a big help. Wrestling gave me an outlet for my anger and my love of sports. It also provided me with an intellectual challenge as well. As we shall see in a later chapter, wrestling is a complex sport that requires intense concentration and a strong competitive spirit. It is also a sport, and the competitors become comrades once they are off the wrestling mat. For me this was very important at that time in my life. The sport provided me with a positive outlet for my anger *and* a wonderful group of friends.

It was thanks to my interest in wrestling that I met Fred Oberlander. Fred was originally from Vienna and he became a mentor and a father figure to me in the sporting world and in business. He was an Olympic wrestler who was at one point the European champion. He was also a member of the International Federation of Wrestling, the world body that governs the sport, which has its head office in Switzerland. Fred and I met not long after I arrived in Montreal. He was in his late thirties, twenty-one years older than me. His wrestling career was just about over at that time but he continued to work out.

Fred Oberlander was able to get out of Austria and go to England before the war with the help of an influential Nazi officer who was also a wrestler. This Nazi officer helped the Oberlander family escape to England* and that is how they survived the war. Fred came to Canada in 1949, a year later than I did. Soon after he arrived he joined the YMHA and became involved in the wrestling program there. He maintained his involvement in the sport for the rest of his life.

He was in the business of supplying material to the shoe industry and he mentored me in business as well as in wrestling. I learned from him that you could be a businessman and an athlete. When I went into business for myself, Fred Oberlander gave me the kind of practical advice I needed, as I had no formal training in the business world.

One of the best pieces of advice he gave me helped me both as a wrestler and as a businessman. At some point during a conversation we were having about wrestling I asked Fred to tell me the best way to get out of a headlock. "Stupid," he said giving me a playful shove, "don't get into it." I've made this one of my life's guiding principles: avoid getting into situations you can't get out of.

Fred Oberlander took me into his home when I was alone in my new country. He had three sons and he treated me like a fourth

* It's curious, isn't it, that this Nazi was able to put his devotion to wrestling and wrestlers ahead of his philosophy of anti-Semitism in this one instance but apparently could not see the humanity in all Jews.

son. He was as proud of my achievements as if he had been my father, and I was grateful for his support. As far as I was concerned he was family and when his sons moved out of Montreal, to Toronto and New York, I took care of him. I assumed the role of caregiver for him until the end of his life. He died in 1993 at the age of eighty-two.

\* \* \*

There was still one element missing from my life during my early days in Canada – romantic love. All of my school friends and most of my family were murdered by the Nazis. Because of the way I had spent the early years of my adolescence I didn't have the opportunity to be a normal teenager, to socialize with friends, to associate with girls my age, and to develop romantic attachments. This all changed when I began working at Montreal Upholstering. It was there that I fell in love for the first time.

Claudette worked on a sewing machine at Montreal Upholstering. She was beautiful, smart, and very nice. She and I had a wonderful relationship. We talked about all kinds of things and generally enjoyed being in one another's company. She inspired me to do my best when I wrestled. Claudette was my first great love.

There was one obvious problem – she wasn't Jewish and I wasn't Catholic. Her father and the rest of her family could not accept me as a suitable mate for her. I hoped that our relationship would continue over time, perhaps leading to marriage and she felt the same way about me. But her family were against any such thing taking place. Her father, two of her brothers, and her uncle worked at Montreal Upholstering, so they knew me and knew me to be a decent fellow but their minds were made up. Her mother was not as adamantly opposed to our union as the other members of her family, but she couldn't convince the others to accept me.

We tried to get her father to see me in a good light. I even went so far as to accompany her to church. We had many conversations about God and religion. But every time the subject of God came up I thought about the babies I had seen tossed into the ditches on my first night at Auschwitz and wondered then, as I do now, about God – how could he allow such behaviour?

Auntie Annie had no problem with my relationship with Claudette. Even though she hoped that I would marry a Jewish girl, she had very positive feelings for Claudette and was happy that I had found someone to be in love with and who loved me in return. Claudette spent a great deal of time at Annie's apartment where I lived. Annie was sensitive enough to our needs to give us privacy, and she always called before she returned home. She was very co-operative and a very smart and caring lady.

Claudette and I had to accept the obvious truth that our relationship would not last forever no matter how much we wanted it to. During what turned out to be our last summer together, I took a trip with her and her parents to Old Orchard Beach in Maine, a popular vacation spot for Quebecers. I was the only one with a car. We had a wonderful vacation but I sensed that Claudette was beginning to see someone else and that this would be our last time together. I realized that when the vacation was over and we got back to Montreal we would have to break our relationship. We had been together for about three years. On the positive side we ended the relationship in as loving a way as possible – without betrayal or acrimony on either side. But it was a very tough time for me emotionally.

Within the year following our break-up, Claudette married a fellow named Richard. They had five children but their marriage ended in divorce. Sadly one of their children committed suicide. Claudette worked at Birks and I saw her there a couple of times. I have to admit that in my memory she was more beautiful than she was in life – but this is probably the case in all situations of a young love that is also the first love. In the end I had to accept that it was probably for the best that we never married. At that time mixed marriages were not common and society was not accepting of them. I was not religious but I was very proud to be a Jew; I had paid a very high price for it and I wanted to pass my heritage on to my children.

In the 1970s I heard the tragic news that Claudette had committed suicide. I went to the funeral in order to pay my respects to her family and to honour all that she meant to me. When we were together we were very happy, and I was saddened to think that something had happened in her life to rob her of her happiness and cause her to take her life. At the funeral one of her daughters came over to me and told me that her mother had always regretted that she didn't marry me. This touched me very deeply and even all these years later there is a small part of my heart that belongs to her.

George and Eleanor's wedding photo, taken at Herzl Hall in Montreal,
8 September 1957.

George, age twenty-five, posing in a wrestler's stance. The photograph was taken in 1957 just prior to the Maccabiah Games.

George carrying the Red Ensign (Canada's flag at the time) at the
Maccabiah Games in 1957, less than ten years after his arrival in Canada.

George's cool, jazz-loving uncle Dennis Komaromi, age twenty-three or twenty-four. The photo was taken by Dennis's uncle, Ignac Komaromi, after the war when Dennis operated a dance studio.

Karci Rothschild, George's best friend. The photo was taken in Budapest, where they met in the orphanage. Karci influenced George's decision to work in the upholstery business.

George and the American wrestler Michael Wittenberg, Maccabiah Games, 1961.

George and Eleanor with their daughters Aviva, Judith, and Marla at the Maccabiah Games in 1969. George was a coach of the Canadian team.

Auntie Annie Pugatch in 1970. Annie rented a room to George in 1949 and became a lifelong friend and positive influence.

George as president of Jaymar. The photo was taken in 1999 before he sold the company.

Wrestlers from across Canada train at the George and Eleanor Reinitz
Wrestling Centre.

George arrived in Canada alone. He and Eleanor now have a family of eighteen members in four generations.

# 5

# Wrestling

As I mentioned in a previous chapter, Nick Sebastian and I used to go to the Y together. When we first started working out there, I was interested in playing soccer and Nick worked out with the wrestlers. He had been involved in the sport in Hungary. I quickly grew tired of soccer because I didn't think that the other members of the team were giving the game their best efforts and I had no patience with anything less than my best. I believed then, and believe now, that everyone should do their best at whatever they do. There was something about wrestling that I found attractive and challenging so I decided to join Nick and the other wrestlers. It turned out this was a fortuitous move – *beschert*, "meant to be," you might say. I immediately loved the sport, as it combined all the elements of the things that interested me.

Wrestling combines the physicality of all sports with the need for mental acuity. Strategy is as important to the sport as physical strength. It is necessary to foresee your opponent's likely next moves in the same way that a chess player, to succeed, must be able to predict what his opponent will do in three or four moves – often before the opponent himself knows what he will do. To me wrestling is a perfect combination of mind and body effort.

The rules of the sport are designed to prevent one opponent from hurting the other during a match, and the match itself is based on a points system. Participants are awarded points based on the holds they execute and avoid. It is possible for a match to end when a wrestler pins his opponent, when he gets both his competitor's shoulders on the mat, but that happens rarely. Evenly matched opponents know how to avoid being pinned.

Nick introduced me to the sport but it was not long before I exceeded his ability in it. This was on way in which I could work toward my goal to do everything I did in my new life in Canada as best I could. This was my goal in my job, and I devoted much the same energy to perfecting my skills as a wrestler.

I trained at the YMCA as well as at the YMHA. It was natural that if I wanted to do my best I should seek out the best trainers in Montreal. The coach at the YMCA was a man by the name of Mr Turnbull. He was also the coach of the wrestling team at McGill University. He needed someone for the McGill team in the light heavyweight division – my weight class – so he put me on the McGill team. I had started to learn English when I arrived in Canada but I didn't speak it very well when Mr Turnbull put me in the red uniform of the university. He told me not to talk to the other wrestlers, especially those on the opposing team. And if any of the wrestlers tried to strike up a conversation and ask me about my field of study, I was to say, "Engineering," so they would think I was in the Engineering Faculty. No matter what I was asked, I would respond, "Engineering." Even if one of the wrestlers asked what the weather was like in Montreal my answer was, "Engineering." The wrestlers must have had a very low opinion of the intelligence of engineers because they never figured out that I wasn't a McGill student and could barely speak English. During the short time I wrestled on the McGill team I attended tournaments at Queen's University and the University of New Brunswick.

I trained and wrestled at the YMHA twice a week. I also joined the Palestre Nationale on Cherrier Street. That was where the best wrestlers in Canada trained. The coach there was a man by the name of Mr Beaulieu. He was very kind to me. He recognized my skill and he gave me a membership to the organization so that I could train with his team. Mr Beaulieu included me with his team and I went to matches in other provinces and in the United States with him. He was the coach of the national team, and I was pleased when he told people he was my trainer. I trained at the Palestre Nationale an additional two times a week.

The coaches at the YMHA were volunteers (Harry Hirschenkoff, for example, was a sewing machine mechanic) who did their best to train and motivate the wrestlers who worked with them. Mr

Turnbull and Mr Beaulieu were professional coaches and they were able to teach me things that I wasn't learning at the YMHA. But wrestling is ultimately an individual sport. When you are on the mat it is just you and your opponent – there is no teammate to cover for you and no goalie to backstop for you. I loved the autonomous nature of the sport; whether I won or lost depended on the decisions I made.

Because it is an individual sport, wrestling requires as much mental preparedness and focus as physical training. The training for the physical aspects of the sport involve both aerobic (street running for speed training, for example) and anaerobic (weight training) elements. Most of a wrestler's time is spent learning the various holds and counter-holds of the sport. It is necessary to practise over and over again to learn all the holds that make up a wrestler's repertoire and it is critical to learn new ones at all times. It is also necessary to learn the counter-holds that will get you out of any situation that a competitor puts you into and to be able to predict how a competing wrestler will respond when you put him in a certain hold. As if all of this was not complicated enough, certain wrestlers develop favourite moves and it is critical to know how to defend against them.

As in all my endeavours I broke wrestling down to its component parts and made certain that I mastered each of them. I devoted as much effort to the psychological aspects of the sport as I did to the physical. I was well aware that my potential opponents were working as hard as I was and I knew that in wrestling, as much as in business, both you and your competitors are looking for advantages and for ways to be in charge. I never made a move until I thought I would succeed; making your opponent wait for your move was a way of indicating your dominance, a way of saying, in effect, "I'm in charge of the mat and because I'm in charge I won't make a move until I am good and ready."

For me there was also a deeper psychological element to wrestling than that of psyching out your opponent. Wrestling helped me cope with the anger I had brought with me to Canada – understandable after all I had been through. The more I became successful at wrestling the more my anger faded away. Wrestlers had to possess both a combative and a co-operative nature and the

wisdom to know which side of our personality to allow to dominate. Because of this I was able to become friendly with wrestlers
I met at competitions. To be clear: the friendship only existed off
the mat. On the mat we were each focused on one thing and one
thing only: victory.

One of the wrestlers I met at the Palestre Nationale was a
Quebecker with the unlikely name of Bob Hornblower. We were
of equal skill and won an equal number of matches. Off the mat
we became very friendly and were happy to spend time with
one another.

One of my opponents with whom I had a harder time forming
a friendship was a German guy from Kitchener, Ontario. He was
the Canadian champion but I saw him as a German. Over time,
however, we became friends. We are still in touch with one another and we reminisce about our matches and who beat whom.
There was no animosity in our competition. For us it was fun, the
joy of competition.

There came a point in my career as a wrestler when I had to
make a choice. If I wanted to continue training at the Palestre
Nationale, Mr Beaulieu expected me to wrestle for his team. But I
was hesitant to desert my friends and coaches at the YMHA. After
all, it was one of the organizations that had welcomed me when I
arrived in Canada and I always felt very much at home there. I was
very proud to be a member of that Jewish organization and to
devote my talents to it. In the end I chose to stay at the YMHA and
I was very successful there. I was on the Y's wrestling team that
competed in provincial, national, and international events. I was
the Quebec Champion in 1952, 1953, and 1954; and I was the
Canadian Champion in 1957–58. I competed for Canada at matches in the United States, and I represented Canada at the Maccabiah Games in Israel in 1957 and 1961.

In 1952 I had the opportunity to wrestle with a man who was
one of my idols in the wrestling world. Henry Wittenburg was an
Olympic champion who had competed in the 1948 games in London, England. I enjoyed the challenge of going against someone I
admired and who was a much better wrestler than I was. It
brought out the best in me. I lost the match but Henry and I
became friends and I learned a great deal from him.

Even though I no longer wrestled with the team from the Palestre Nationale, I competed at its facility, representing the YMHA. In 1954 or thereabouts I was competing at the Palestre Nationale against one of their better wrestlers, Georges Ficheau. After I won the match, his fans demonstrated their displeasure by means of what I took to be anti-Semitic comments. A priest who was at the match took the microphone and calmed the crowd. That was about the only time I sensed any anti-Semitism at the Palestre Nationale.

I have long suspected that the people who attended this match at the Palestre Nationale were used to the kind of wrestling they saw at the Montreal Forum, which was more entertainment than sport. In those matches it was considered acceptable to throw chairs and anything else that came to hand, and the spectators were used to voicing their approval or disapproval. The people at the Palestre Nationale were unused to Olympic-style wrestling (a sport that dates from the classical Greek Olympics) and were probably expressing themselves in order to generate more excitement. In Olympic-style wrestling the goal is not to hurt your opponent but to outperform him. More generally, I don't think that the fans at the Palestre National saw me as a Jew; they saw me as a foreigner. However – and I well remember these feelings from that time – if anyone had called me a dirty Jew I was more than prepared to fight and I was definitely prepared to fight dirty.

In 1956 I was in excellent physical condition, the best shape I had ever been in and I was able to beat any competitor in Canada. Unfortunately I accidently broke my finger while training a younger, less-experienced wrestler. My hand was in a cast for a long time and I was unable to train while it healed. When my finger recovered I competed in the trials for the 1956 Olympics but lost to Bob Steckle, the Canadian champion. I fought a spirited fight and was ahead of my competitor on points until the very end of the match, when he bested me. I attributed my loss to the fact that I hadn't been able to train for such a long period. This loss was a devastating blow to me because I was in such excellent physical condition that I believed I could have bested any competitor.

Nick and I were saving our money so that we would be able to go into business for ourselves. I was so confident that I would be able to win the Olympic trials and represent Canada at the games in Sydney, Australia, that our plan was to launch our business following the 1956 games, held in November and December. Because I was unable to compete in the Olympics we decided to start our business in July of that year.

Even if Nick and I had postponed going into business until after the games as we had originally planned. I now realize I had no guarantee that he would have maintained his interest while I was away. When I had gone to Ontario to work on the tobacco harvest all those years before, Nick had given up our room, leaving me without a place to live when I returned. I couldn't have been sure he wouldn't have done something similar while I was competing in Australia. As it turned out, not being able to compete in the 1956 Olympics probably worked out for the best.

Even though I devoted a great deal of energy to my business once we had started it up, I continued to train, and in 1957 I won the trials allowing me to compete for Canada at the Commonwealth Games. This time I beat Bob Steckle, the man who had defeated me in 1956. Sadly, I was unable to attend the Commonwealth Games because they were held in Cardiff, Wales, and it would have meant being absent from home for too long while Eleanor was pregnant with our first child. In those days air travel was too expensive and the ocean voyage to Wales would have taken a week each way plus three weeks at the games. I couldn't see myself leaving Eleanor for that length of time. Also, it would have meant being absent from the business for as much as five weeks. Nick needed me in order to ensure that it was well managed. Bob Steckle went in my place and won the gold medal in wrestling at the Commonwealth Games.

I continued to train while working full time and enjoying my new role as a father. My last competition was at the 1961 Maccabiah Games. I *almost* won the gold medal. My opponent, Michael Wittenberg, the son of gold-medallist Henry Wittenberg, and I were tied on points and the rule at the time was that in the event of a tie the lighter wrestler was declared the winner. Wittenberg was a fraction lighter than I was so he won the gold and I took home the silver.

I ended my career as a wrestler with mixed emotions. On the one hand it meant that I would not be under pressure to train and compete while I was preoccupied with my business and my family. On the other hand there is always a little regret when one chapter of life finishes and another begins.

Although I no longer competed in wrestling matches, I continued to encourage the sport and I served as a coach of the wrestling team at the Snowdon YMHA on Westbury Avenue. I coached there and worked out with the young wrestlers until I was fifty-seven years old, at which time I traded my wrestling singlet for golf shoes and took up golf. I never stopped supporting wrestling, and contributed funds so that the YMHA team would have the necessary equipment for it to train and compete. I did this until the Y stopped offering the sport owing to a lack of space.

Most of the characteristics that make for a successful athlete, especially one like me who successfully competed internationally, are the same characteristics that make for success in business. In my business career as in my athletic career I competed at a high level in the international arena. In fact, as we shall see later in this book, it was more than my competitive nature that led to my success. It was also my co-operative temperament that, in a very tough business situation, brought me a very positive benefit.

Because wrestling brought so much to my life, I wanted to share its benefits with others. I was pleased to share my business success with the YMHA, and donated a wrestling facility to it in the year 2001. Eleanor and I contributed the funds to construct a building so that wrestling, long absent from the Y, would return. What is more, I was able to convince Viktor Zilberman, a top-calibre Russian wrestler, to sign on as coach.

I first met Viktor when he came to Canada from Russia via Israel in the mid-seventies, probably in 1973. At that time he barely spoke any English but he was able to land a coaching job in Thunder Bay, Ontario. He later returned to Montreal to work as a coach of the provincial wrestling team. In the short time he had been in Canada, he had trained many Olympic athletes for his new country and he became the official coach for the Olympic Wrestling team. He also accepted a teaching and coaching position at Vanier College in 1978.

When Viktor returned to Montreal we renewed our acquaintance and it didn't take us long to become close friends. He and I talked for many years about re-establishing a wrestling program at the YMHA. It disturbed us both that the Y had discontinued the wrestling program many years earlier, for lack of space. Historically, wrestling was an important part of the Y, and its program had produced many national champions. (Photographs of YMHA champion wrestlers lined the main corridor of the old Davis Y building on Mount Royal Avenue for many years until the building was sold to the Université de Montréal.)

The general public knows very little about wrestling. The average citizen, even those who do not follow sport, knows something about hockey or football or basketball, but not about wrestling. Wrestling demands training and dedication from its participants in the way that all sport does. But wrestling requires an added level of determination because the competitor has no team members to rely on. A wrestler must focus totally on the competition and be in excellent physical condition or he will not win his match – and he will have no one to blame but himself.

I believe that wrestling is a great way to teach young people how to compete and to be physically fit. I believe that young people trained in the sport of wrestling are able to carry the skills it takes to be a successful wrestler into their future endeavours – no matter what they are – and contribute to their success in them. Because Viktor agreed to participate in the program, I agreed to provide the financing.

I have to admit that even though I had Viktor's support I was still nervous that I would spend a lot of money on a building for a sport that had no participants. Viktor's mother, Mrs Zilberman, was the one who helped me understand that if there was a good wrestling facility and it had a good coach, it would soon be filled with good wrestlers. She illustrated her belief with a story about a deserted square in Tel Aviv near where she lived. It was barren and lifeless. When the city landscaped it and planted some trees, birds (and children) came to the park and it became a very lively place. This was her way of saying, "If you build it they will come." And she proved to be correct. We built the Reinitz Wrestling Centre and young people came to it to train for the sport.

This program at the Y was so successful that in 2006 I offered it the opportunity to build a wrestling centre at the summer camp it operated in the Laurentians. I wanted to introduce the youngsters who attended the camp to the sport. Every year I pay to have one of the young wrestlers who train at the centre act as a coach at the camp.

The program I endowed is very successful and I am thrilled that it has four professional coaches working under Viktor's supervision to nurture young wrestlers. The provincial and federal governments also contribute to the centre, demonstrating its importance to Quebec and to Canada. More than a hundred young people train at the centre. As well as Montrealers we have youngsters from all over the world. Kids from Russia, Israel, Iran, and many other countries come to attend school in Montreal so they can train at the Reinitz Wrestling Centre. And the wrestling team competes worldwide. Wrestling gives these kids a common purpose and I am pleased to say that for the first decade or so of the twenty-first century our team has been very successful in developing world champions and Olympians.

I consider it my good fortune to be able to help all the young boys and girls who come to train in the sport of wrestling. I am especially proud of the youth of Canada who train at the Reinitz Centre and go on to become good and productive Canadian citizens. I am just as proud of all the other young people from all different nations, languages, and religions who train there. The sport of wrestling breeds a friendship and camaraderie among these kids that transcends the kind of conflict their differences might engender in other contexts. They compete while on the wrestling mat but they are devoted to one another when off it.

\* \* \*

I had to give up competitive wrestling in part because of an ill-timed minor injury but mostly because the time I devoted to my family and my business didn't leave much leisure for the sport. I did, however, continue to train as often as I could. It was my way of staying healthy and centred.

In the early 1990s an opportunity presented itself in an odd and unexpected way for me to demonstrate that I still had the skill and spirit of a wrestler. At that time the national team from the former

Soviet Republic of Georgia, which included a number of World and Olympic medalists, came to Montreal to train with Viktor for a couple of days before continuing on to New York, their final destination. I invited Viktor and the Georgian team to come to the Jaymar factory in Terrebonne for a visit, during which members of the team, along with some of the YMHA wrestlers, would put on a demonstration for the Jaymar employees.

I had a wrestling area prepared with mats that I had stored at the factory, and at a certain point in the afternoon I halted production and had the employees gather for the demonstration and an explanation of the sport of wrestling at the Olympic level. The employees enjoyed the demonstration and I found myself caught up in the fun. After the final match I stepped into the middle of the mat and asked if any of my employees would like to have a wrestling match with me. I was over fifty at the time and not dressed for a wrestling match, but I did remove my suit jacket.

One of my employees, a strong young fellow in his thirties, accepted the challenge and joined me on the mat. Viktor, the wrestlers, and my employees seemed nervous that I would be bested and embarrassed by the young fellow. I had full confidence that this wouldn't be the case and I allowed my competitor to attack. Training and experience will out, and I was able to throw the fellow onto the mat in a match that lasted less than half a minute.

All in attendance enjoyed the occasion and I derived great pleasure not from beating a much younger man but because I still had the ability to participate in the sport I loved.

# 6

# George and Eleanor

By 1955, after I'd been in Canada for seven years, my life had taken on the appearance of normality. I say, the *appearance* of normality, because the memories of the friends and especially of my family whom I had lost during the *Shoah* were still very much a part of my thoughts. But I was also developing solid relations with friends in Montreal, notably with Zoltan and Nick, and especially with Auntie Annie. In every possible way they became my family. The anger that had been such a part of my life from the time I left Auschwitz was beginning to abate. This change was due in large part to my participation in the sport of wrestling and to Auntie Annie's role and influence in my life. On the surface I looked like a regular twenty-three-year-old bachelor. I was interested in girls and I had a large group of friends with whom I shared a social life.

All the other immigrants with whom I was friendly were, like me, enjoying life in our new country. Most of us had started to work hard almost from the moment our feet touched Canadian soil. We enjoyed the freedom to do what we wished without fear and we also believed that hard work would lead to success. That belief, so long absent from our lives in Europe, motivated us to live life to the fullest. To that end we, the survivors and other immigrants who had arrived in Canada in 1948, formed a club at the YMHA. We referred to it as the 48ers Club. It was essentially a social club and we had dances and parties and other similar events. It was not an exclusive club and many of the people who participated in our events were Montreal Jews from all walks of life.

At one of the 48ers' parties I met a girl called Anna whom I found very attractive. I was looking for a girlfriend, and thought it

was time to think seriously about getting married. In those days
people got married in their early twenties. I very much enjoyed
Anna's company and we always had a good time together. There
was one problem in my relationship with her, however, and that was
her mother. Anna's mother was very protective – over-protective
actually – of her. She was worried that Anna and I would have sex
and so she kept an eye on us wherever and whenever she could.
Her mother was right, of course; Anna and I *were* having sex. Her
mother's watchful eye made it difficult for us but not impossible.
Anna had an older sister who was married with a child and we
would babysit for her. And that is where we would have sex – when
we were babysitting for her sister. I liked Anna very much but I
also knew that as much as I liked her she was not the person with
whom I wanted to raise a family and to spend the rest of my life.

To celebrate the arrival of 1956, one of the members of the 48ers
Club hosted a New Year's Eve party at their house. The party was
held in the west end of Montreal on Mackenzie Street. This was a
slightly more affluent part of the city than the St Lawrence area
where I had been living before I met Auntie Annie. But it was not
so affluent that it was out of the reach of the new arrivals to Montreal who were beginning to make their way in their new city.
Anna, eighteen at the time, was of course my date for the party.
Unfortunately her overbearing mother gave her a curfew and she
had to be home very soon after midnight, just as 1955 turned into
1956 and the party was still going strong.

I knew that my relationship with Anna would not last into the
New Year. As much as I wanted to get married, I knew that Anna
would not be the person for me. She was very nice and we had a
good time together but she was she was too much under her mother's interfering thumb and I very much prized my independence.

While we were at the party I noticed a very attractive woman
who was there with a date. In the course of the evening I had the
opportunity to talk to her, and learned that her name was Eleanor
Schwartz and that she was on a first date with Willy Klein, the guy
who had brought her to the party. Willy was a friend of mine and
a fellow member of the 48ers Club.

I had to leave the party in order to take Anna home and I asked
Nick, also a member of the 48ers Club and also at the party, to keep

an eye on Willy and make certain that Willy drank enough to make him incapable of driving Eleanor home. My immediate impression of Eleanor was that she was a very happy person but also one with good common sense, and I knew that she would never get into a car with someone who was inebriated.

My scheme worked out exactly as planned. When I got back to the party after taking Anna home, I noticed that Willy was much too drunk to even consider driving and I started talking to Eleanor again. I didn't know and didn't care if she'd seen that I had been with Anna, had taken her home, and then returned alone to the party. I pointed out to her that Willy was in no condition to drive and I would be more than happy to take her home when she was ready to leave. I made sure to stick close to her for the rest of the night so that none of the other guys could make a move on her.

When the time came to leave I drove her home in the car Nick and I owned together and on her doorstep I told her that one day she and I would be married. She clearly thought I was crazy. She barely knew me; we had only met a couple of hours earlier at a party that she only attended because her girlfriends pressured her into accepting a blind date. She didn't say that she thought I was out of my mind, but she didn't have to – the look she gave me said it all.

What Eleanor didn't know – what she couldn't know – was that I was the type of person who was determined to turn what seemed like an impulsive New Year's prediction into a reality. My comment certainly seemed rash at the time. If 1955 had been a very busy year for me, 1956 would likely be even more hectic. Nick and I were firming up the plans for our business and I had every intention of continuing to train and participate in the Olympics. Even if Eleanor didn't realize it then, the statement I made on her doorstep early in the morning of the first day of 1956, one of the coldest days of the winter, was sincere.

In spite of my doorstep prediction, I didn't see Eleanor again until late that year. I was very involved with my business and with wrestling, and I really had little time for anything else. But I never forgot Eleanor and I knew that as soon as I was able I would find her again and rekindle our relationship. As foolish as I may have appeared to her when I took her home on that cold night, I sensed that Eleanor was not looking for a serious relationship at that time and that the best thing I could do to ensure my chances with her would be to give her some space. I had a lot to accomplish in the first part of the year 1956, so that worked well for me.

Over the course of the winter I ran into Willy periodically and I asked him if he was still dating Eleanor. He told me that he wasn't dating her anymore. In fact, he had only had that one date with her on New Year's Eve and I made certain that his date had come to an abrupt end. I asked him if he would give me Eleanor's phone number, but he didn't have it. This didn't deter me because I knew that Eleanor and I had another friend in common – a woman named Yvonne.

Like me, Yvonne was originally from Hungary. She had survived the war in Paris and had also come to Canada in 1948. Yvonne was a part of the group of friends who formed the 48ers Club and she had also attended the New Year's Eve party on Mackenzie Street.

At the end of November 1956, I called Yvonne and asked her for Eleanor's phone number. She was reluctant to give me the phone number, as she didn't know how Eleanor felt about me. But she did offer to have both Eleanor and me over to her house for a dinner party. This was a more relaxed and informal way for us to meet again after I hadn't spoken to her for almost a year. Yvonne filled me in on Eleanor's background. At the time Eleanor lived with her family on Clanranald Avenue. Yvonne interpreted that to mean that Eleanor came from a wealthy family because, as Yvonne put it, the area was "almost in Hampstead," one of Montreal's wealthiest suburbs.

Following the dinner party at Yvonne's, Eleanor and I started to go out together regularly in order to get to know one another. After having dated for a while, I asked her to go to the New Year's Eve party with me that year. This time, Eleanor was *my* date for the evening and I didn't have to resort to trickery to drive her home! Following that date, which saw 1956 become 1957, our relationship became more serious, and in the fall of that year we decided to become engaged, planning to get married in late 1957 or early 1958.

Eleanor was from a large family. She had three brothers, two of whom were older than her and one younger. Because she was the only daughter in the family, her father and her brothers spoiled her. In addition, her brothers and her parents, especially her father, also acted as her protector in that they insisted that she follow the social *mores* of the day, which were much more rigid in the mid-1950s than they are today. This meant that pre-marital sex was not an option.

Eleanor's extended family was also quite large. She had several aunts and uncles, and I found it appealing to be a part of a large family, especially a large Jewish family. I was not in any way religious but I was proud of my heritage. My Jewish background was very important to us both, and Eleanor's family made me feel part of a Jewish community.

Ten years later, in 1966, Eleanor and I were on vacation in California and spent some time with Yvonne, who was by then living there with her second husband. In the course of our visit, Yvonne said, "If I had known how successful George would become I would have kept him for myself." I was flattered by her good-natured kibitzing – I'm not sure her husband (or Eleanor) felt the same way.

Eleanor was sexy and good-looking but much to my disappointment she refused to have sex with me. In those days women were considered "cheap" if they had sex before marriage and Eleanor's reputation meant a lot to her. As much as I wanted to have sex with her, I respected her for adamantly holding to her values. I admired that strength and believed it was a good quality to have.

As our relationship developed I introduced Eleanor to my love of wrestling and she would periodically attend events to watch me compete. In the spring of 1957, after we had been going out for a few months, she came to watch me wrestle at the Paul Sauvé Arena. I was aware, of course, of the strong connection that Eleanor and I by then had with one another, but something happened at the wrestling match that showed me how strong that connection truly was. Eleanor was so affected by my effort on the mat that she fainted.

I saw medics in the area where I knew she was sitting, but I couldn't see much else – and in any event I was focused on the match, which I won. I found out later that the commotion in the stands was due to the fact that Eleanor had passed out. My reputation as a "player" was such that those who knew me opined that she had fainted because she was pregnant. Nothing could have been further from the truth!

Eleanor and I were planning to become engaged in September 1957 and to get married before the end of the year. But in May 1957 I won the honour of representing Canada in the Maccabiah Games to be held in Israel in September 1957. I thought it would be a good idea to get married before the games, spend our honeymoon in Israel, and then travel around Europe. This would give Eleanor the opportunity to meet my cousins who lived in Israel. Eleanor's father had booked the Herzl Hall for our wedding, and changing the date meant that he would have to change those arrangements. Luckily he was able to do that, and Eleanor and I were married on 8 September 1957. It was a large wedding officiated by Rabbi Denberg, who somehow had learned a lot about me and made some very flattering comments during the ceremony. Two days later we flew to Israel.

The advantage of combining our honeymoon with the Maccabiah Games was that my airfare was paid by the Canadian team that was attending the games. The flight from Canada to Israel took thirty-eight hours with many stopovers. We had layovers in Newfoundland, Iceland, England, and a couple of other European countries before we reached Tel Aviv. At each stop we would get off the plane and the athletes would do some warm-up exercises in order to make the trip more bearable and help us keep in shape for the games.

Upon arriving in Israel we stayed with the Canadian contingent in the athletes' village. For the first couple of nights Eleanor and I lived in separate tents in the village. Israel had acquired (taken, really) the tents in Egypt following the 1956 war. I slept in the men's section and Eleanor in the women's. There was no indoor plumbing and for the first time in her life Eleanor had to use a latrine – itself an experience for a spoiled, middle-class girl from Montreal. After a couple of nights of roughing it in the tents, she moved in with my cousin who lived in Tel Aviv. Eleanor spent her days with me but there was a 9:00 p.m. curfew for the athletes, and at that time she had to return to my cousin's home. Living with my cousin provided a real challenge for Eleanor as they didn't speak the same language – but she was a good sport about it and made the best of the situation. Unquestionably this was a most unique honeymoon.

Marrying Eleanor and competing in the Maccabiah Games made 1957 the best year of my life. I was in excellent physical condition, at my competitive best. Even more important, I was chosen by the other athletes on the Canadian team to be the flag bearer at the games. It is common for the flag bearer to be a member of a country's wrestling team, as that sport traces its origins to the ancient Greek Olympics. The honour of carrying the flag was extremely moving for me, and I found myself on the verge of shedding tears of joy and pride. Somehow, I was able to channel these emotions into a great big smile that expressed my happiness at all that I had achieved since I arrived in Canada nine short years previously.

With great pride and great emotion I carried the flag of my beloved new country into the stadium in Israel, the world's newest country, a country I also loved. My friend and mentor Fred Oberlander taught me how to carry the flag (which is not as easy as it looks) and to dip it in homage to the Israeli dignitaries, most of whom were the country's pioneers and included David Ben-Gurion.

The emotion of that moment was overwhelming to me. Thirteen years earlier I had been a victim of Hitler's attempt to rid the world of Jews and now, here I was, carrying the Canadian flag in a country founded by Jews for Jews. If I could have done it I would have knelt and kissed the earth of Israel. But there is only one way to carry a flag and that is to stand tall – and to stand taller still while dipping it to honour the VIPs in the reviewing stand.

Only the births of our children came close to giving me the feelings of love and pride that I felt that day, honouring the state of Israel, its leadership, and Eleanor.

The wrestling competitions were held in Ramat Gun, a satellite town of Tel Aviv a little to its east. The temperature was almost 40 degrees Celsius and the wrestling mats were made of quilted straw. All in all these were the most uncomfortable conditions I had ever wrestled in. But my enthusiasm at competing in a Jewish country could not be diminished by a little discomfort. I won the silver medal, losing the gold to Max Olman of South Africa, one of the best wrestlers in the world at that time.

Following the games we travelled in Europe for three more weeks. In order to afford the honeymoon I had to borrow $500* from the business that Nick and I had opened the year previously.

---

* The equivalent of around $4,300 in 2017.

The opportunity to compete in the Maccabiah Games with Eleanor in the stands motivating me to excel, and to then travel around Europe was worth every penny. It was a joyous and memorable way for us to begin our life together.

* * *

I don't think that even I knew how accurate my prediction was on that cold early morning in January 1956 that Eleanor and I would be married. I know that I saw a beautiful and lively woman, but I also must have recognized, even at our first meeting, something of the inner qualities that made her such a good wife and life partner.

I wasn't aware of it back then – and neither was Eleanor – but we had certain fundamental things in common. We had both come through love affairs with a mature sense of what we wanted in a mate and what we wanted from life. The emotional scars we bore from these experiences soon healed, leaving no real scar tissue. We were quickly able to form a strong emotional bond with one another that has lasted a very long time and continues to be strong. I sometimes joke that if I had married someone with a less strong personality than Eleanor my life would have been easier. But in truth it is her strength of character, her ability to stand up for herself and challenge me when she sees fit, that has been at the core of our successful marriage.

Over the years I have come to rely heavily on her ability to judge people clearly and accurately. Her advice has prevented me from making costly mistakes in business and in life generally. She has an innate ability to determine when someone is genuinely worthy of doing business with or needs a helping hand, and when this is not the case.

I didn't know at the time that Eleanor hadn't wanted to attend that first New Year's Eve party, but I'm thrilled that she did!

# 7

# Jaymar, 1956–1980

I had known from a very early age that I would one day go into business for myself. When I was a youngster some of my happiest moments were spent working with my father, and I learned from him how to run a business and how to treat the people who worked for you. I was a born risk taker with a strong entrepreneurial instinct. Even the Nazis, during the time I was incarcerated in Auschwitz could not, try as they might, crush this spirit out of me.

When I finally decided that I was ready to operate my own furniture factory, my first thought was to approach Sydney and Leonard Friedman, my bosses at Montreal Upholstering, to see if they could be persuaded to offer me a partnership in the company. They were, respectively, the sons of Max and his brother Ben Friedman, the two founders of the business. Max and Ben were getting ready to retire and have their sons take over. I became the foreman when I was eighteen years old, reporting to Sydney Friedman. After seven years I was practically running the place. I did whatever was asked of me to the best of my ability, working as hard as if I owned the business.

Neither Sydney nor Leonard was all that interested in running the business. They tended to work half days and devote the rest of their time to other pursuits such as golf. For a business like Montreal Upholstering to be successful, at least one of the owners had to be in the factory at all times to keep an eye on production to ensure that things were running smoothly and to maintain the quality of the product. That is the way the elder Friedmans had built and operated the business. I approached Sydney and Leonard and proposed that I be given something more than my salary – that because of my contribution to the success of the business I might be given some equity. They told me that would not be possible. So I replied that I would start my own business. "Go ahead," they said. "Do what you want." They also told me that others had tried to do exactly the same thing and had ended up coming back to try to get their old jobs back. These "others" to whom they referred obviously didn't have my drive and ambition. In a way I was surprised that they didn't recognize this quality in me after benefiting from it for so many years. In any event, they underestimated me when they thought I would fail if I went into business for myself. They made the mistake of not taking me seriously.

Nick and I had been talking about starting our own business for some time. Our first idea was to buy a truck and, like my father, go into the trucking business. We were young and strong and felt confident that we could handle any job that came our way. But we quickly discarded that idea and we talked about going into the furniture business. I had experience running a factory and I had pretty good contacts with both retailers and suppliers. After the Friedman cousins refused to take me into their business as a partner, Nick and I decided to open our own factory.

Auntie Annie was a very important part of the discussions that led to the founding of Jaymar. In fact it was she who came up with the name. Nick's and my mother's names were both Marta and my father's name was Jacob. Auntie put the two names together and came up with Jaymar. Moreover, Auntie had savings of five thousand dollars, which she invested in the business. She had worked as a bookkeeper and had managed to save that amount of money. Before the war she had worked for a German company named Scherling with an office in Montreal, but she quit when Hitler's picture went up in the lunchroom.

Nick and I had each managed to save $1,700, so the total start-up investment in Jaymar was $8,400.* In addition to lending us money so that we could start our business, Auntie took care of our books in the evening after she had already worked a full day at her regular job.

* The equivalent of roughly $76,000 in 2017 dollars.

Having learned all aspects of the furniture business while I was at Montreal Upholstering, I knew the suppliers from whom to buy the raw materials, the shops to which we could sub-contract the construction of the frames, and the retailers to whom we could sell our furniture. I quit my job at Montreal Upholstering and we started up our business in the summer of 1956.

Nick stayed on at his job as a shipper for Mirado Children's Wear. We were both single and didn't need much money to live on, so we split Nick's salary between us. He earned somewhere in the neighbourhood of sixty dollars a week so we were each able to live on thirty dollars a week. At that time we both lived with Auntie and our rent for room and board was fifteen dollars a week each, so that left fifteen dollars to spend on ourselves. When you figure that a family was probably living on less than eighty dollars a week at that time, we weren't doing too badly.

One of the suppliers to the furniture industry was a company called Plastic Coated Textiles. This company carried a full line of products, including hammers, upholstering tacks and nails – everything we needed, except (in spite of the company's name) textiles, to outfit a factory devoted to the manufacture of furniture. One of the owners of the company, Harry Feldman, told me that he would supply our company and that he would help us in any way he could. Harry was the first person to extend us credit, and I remember him with gratitude for that.

There were six or seven stores on St Hubert and one in Lachine called Lachine Home Furniture, to which I believed we could sell the furniture we manufactured. In addition to these stores there were probably another three or four retailers with whom I had good relations. The owners of all these stores were Jewish and I would feel comfortable calling on them when the time came.

I also thought that the time was right for Nick and me to strike out on our own because I anticipated that the furniture industry was about to undergo an important change and I wanted to get in on the ground floor. I had read an article in a magazine about sofa beds. Because apartments in New York City were small, a sofa bed gave renters what amounted to an extra room. At that time Simmons was the only manufacturer of sofa beds under the brand name Hide-A-Bed, and the retailer Castro Convertibles was doing very well with them. In order to capitalize on this new trend in home furnishings, I created the name Make-A-Bed, and I was determined to manufacture a line of sofa beds under that name.

The Simmons product was very weighty and bulky, made from angle iron, which was a very heavy material. In Waterloo, Ontario, there was a factory called Waterloo Springs that manufactured all sorts of swivels, springs, and mechanical things for the furniture industry. One of the key people in that company was a German engineer who was in charge of designing and developing new products. I got in touch with him and convinced him to design and produce a mechanism that would allow a sofa to be opened into a bed similar to the way the Simmons Hide-A-Bed worked, but I wanted him to make the mechanism lighter and more pleasing to the eye. He was able to create just such a product and it was made out of a material that we could paint so that it was colourful and therefore more attractive. Waterloo Springs agreed to give us the exclusive rights to this mechanism for six months. After that, the company would have the right to sell the invention to other furniture manufacturers.

Nick and I rented a small factory space, about fifteen hundred square feet, at 957 Amherst about two kilometres from the Montreal Upholstering factory on Mentana Street. Our proximity to my former employer meant that some of its employees could come to work for Jaymar in the evenings or on weekends after their regular shift at Montreal Upholstering. The employees from Montreal Upholstering were very loyal to me and were pleased to earn extra money by helping us out. Among the people who came to work for us in the evenings were Claudette's husband, Richard, and her father and her brother.

I was pleased to have the assistance of the experienced employees from Montreal Upholstering for several reasons. We had worked together for a long time and having my colleagues with me made the transition from employee to employer easier. I felt that if my fellow workers from Montreal Upholstering had faith in me, it was a sign that the decision to form my own company was the correct one. At the same time, as much as I enjoyed working with friends from my former workplace, I knew that we needed our own staff who would work for Jaymar on a full-time basis.

We at first thought that one of the advantages of having Nick keep his job at Mirado was that he could "borrow" thread from the factory for us to use in our business. However, thread used to manufacture children's pyjamas is not suitable for the textiles used in the manufacture of furniture. The furniture we made with this thread was returned to us because the stitching unravelled. We learned from this that if we wanted to manufacture a quality product there was no way we could cut corners on the purchase of supplies.

While we worked to get our factory organized to make sofa beds, we manufactured rocking chairs, which were very popular at that time. The rocking chair we built was less bulky than those of other manufacturers. It was a sleeker more modern product – if you can consider a rocking chair modern in any way.

Very soon after we opened our factory we received the first mechanism from the Waterloo Springs company and we switched over to the manufacture of sofa beds under the brand name Make-A-Bed. In order to help retailers sell the sofa beds we created a large poster showing the six different Make-A-Bed models. Attached to each poster were samples of the fabrics the consumer could choose from. Eleanor's mother wanted a job so that she could earn some extra money; I paid her to glue the fabric samples to the posters.

I looked after manufacturing and, thanks to my knowledge of the retail customers for furniture in Montreal, I took care of sales as well. Nick handled the administrative side of things, looking after payroll and the other managerial details that occurred daily. Auntie Annie came in to work two days a week to give him a hand.

We had a well-designed product that met the needs of people living in small apartments and the growing families of the post-war Baby Boom. The other growth industry of that period was the automobile industry. Now that the war was over and materials were available, cars underwent a design revolution. I copied our furniture designs from the look of the tail fins of the new cars that were coming on the market. We made a flared, rounded arm on one of our lines that looked like the tail fins of a Chevrolet and gave the product the name Impala. Our business took off very quickly.

We had to be careful with our money so we bought fabric only as we needed it. Buying in small quantities meant that we weren't getting our supplies for the best price. The frames came from small millwright shops. We manufactured the cushions, which in those days were made by wrapping three-inch springs in felt and covering them in fabric. The cushions were made in much the same way as mattresses. The upholstering, which included sewing the fabric, was also done at our shop on Amherst Street. It wasn't long before we had to take more space to keep up with the demand for our furniture. Nick and I handled some deliveries with our jointly owned car. We would strap a sofa bed to the top of the car and by some miracle we never had an accident and at no time did a sofa bed fall off the roof.

We were embarrassed that we didn't have a proper delivery van, so we would park the car away from the store we were delivering to, and Nick and I would carry the sofa bed to the store. Being young strong guys, we didn't mind carrying our product ourselves. We pretended it made us look more professional to deliver in this way.

By 1957 we were able to buy a second-hand pick-up truck. We used it to make the deliveries and we also used it when we went out with friends. We put benches in the back of the truck and our friends would sit there when we took them out to dinner or to the movies. The tailgate didn't work all that well – it didn't always stay in the upright position – and I was pleased that none of our furniture, or any of our friends, ever fell off the truck.

One day, while I was on a sales call to one of our customers, Vezina Furniture, on St Lawrence Boulevard, I met a sales agent who carried a line of kitchen sets. His name was Roger Hébert. He asked if he could add our sofa bed line to the products he sold. He told me that all he needed was a photograph of the sofa bed along with some fabric samples and he would be able to sell them. I liked the idea of getting professional sales help, so we made a deal that Roger would get a 5 percent commission on all the sales he generated.

At that time one of the three major department stores in Montreal was Morgan's (now called La Baie). Roger convinced the furniture buyer at Morgan's to carry one of our sofa beds on a consignment basis. He promised the buyer that if it didn't sell we would take it back, so there was no risk to the retailer. He didn't tell us how the deal was structured; he only told us that he had sold a Make-A-Bed to Morgan's. We delivered the product believing we had a firm sale. On the weekend following our delivery, when Roger was certain that the sofa bed was on display, he sent his wife to the store to buy it.

A few days later Roger went to see the buyer, ostensibly to ensure that the Make-A-Bed had arrived and that it was displayed on the sales floor. Obviously the product was no longer there, as it had been removed for delivery to Roger's home. Feigning innocence, Roger asked the buyer where the Make-A-Bed was. With an emphatic snap of his fingers, the buyer told him it had sold over the weekend. Roger was suitably impressed and convinced the buyer to place an order for six Make-A-Beds. This time he took the trouble to get a written order without any return privileges.

Roger then went up and down St Lawrence, showing the furniture merchants on that street the written order that Morgan's had purchased six Make-A-Beds. If they wanted to be competitive, he said, they should buy them as well. Here was the proof of the deal with Morgan's.

One of the retailers he sold a sofa bed to was a furniture retailer by the name of Faucher Electrique. When Roger went back to the store to see if the product had sold, one of the salesmen told him that it was unsellable because it was broken. Roger quickly got the message that if we didn't pay *spiff* (a bribe) under the table to the salesmen they would sabotage the sale of the product by breaking it and telling any customer who showed an interest in it that it wasn't a good product because it broke too easily. We learned our lesson and made sure to take care of the salesmen who would be selling our furniture.

As our sales were growing very quickly, business at Montreal Upholstering, my former employer, was declining. And as its business decreased more and more of its skilled employees were anxious to join Jaymar. The employees and I had developed a very good working relationship and they were pretty sure they would have a good future with my company.

About two and a half years after Nick and I started Jaymar Furniture, Montreal Upholstering filed for bankruptcy. At that time I hired Sydney Friedman, my former boss who had refused to give me a share in his company, to work in sales for Jaymar. He brought his experience to our company and worked for us for about twenty years, up until his retirement.

Every business has difficulties in its early years and Jaymar was no different in this respect. I expected problems to arise and I was confident that I could solve them. But in 1959 Jaymar experienced an unexpected setback that I resolved in an unanticipated way. Late one night in the fall of that year, just as Eleanor and I were getting ready for bed, we turned on the radio to listen to the late news. We heard a report that a four-alarm fire had broken out in a factory building on Amherst Street. I knew from the description of the building on the news that it was the building where Jaymar was located.

I dressed quickly and sped to the factory, arriving just as a ladder was being raised to the window of our office. The ladder broke the window. I was a healthy young man of twenty-six and, as the reader already knows, I was also more than a little foolhardy. I climbed onto the fire truck and climbed up the ladder to our office. The firemen on the ground were yelling at me to get down but I pretended I didn't hear them. I wanted to get into the office and rescue the company's books. I had no idea who owed us money and how much they owed us, and I wanted the ledgers in order to collect the amounts owed. We were not in a position to write off any amount, much less risk our entire accounts receivable.

Once I had the ledgers in my arms I didn't take the chance of going down the way I came up. I knew that the firemen were waiting for me. The building had an exterior fire escape on the side of the building opposite to where the fire equipment had been set up and I went down that way.

As it turned out, most of the damage to our factory was caused by smoke and water. The firemen sprayed water everywhere. Fortunately we were insured and the insurance adjuster we hired settled our claim in such a way that we didn't lose any money. In fact, if I remember correctly we probably made a little money on the claim. The adjuster told me that he had never heard of a businessman going up a fireman's ladder to get into a burning building to rescue his company's books. I had been a risk taker even before I started stealing potato skins in Auschwitz to feed my father and myself, and going into a burning building didn't seem all that dangerous to me.

In 1960 Ben Friedman, one of the brothers who had founded Montreal Upholstering and Leonard's father, got in touch with me and offered to rent us space in their building on Mentana Street. Thanks to the growth of our business, we were in a position to use more manufacturing space; it would allow us to add sofas and other living room furniture to our product line in addition to the Make-A-Beds. In addition, most of our employees lived in that neighbourhood, so we took Ben up on his offer.

So, when our lease on Amherst Street expired we took over the Montreal Upholstering space on Mentana near the corner of Rachel. We occupied most of the building but there was one other tenant: Montreal Frame, a company that manufactured the wooden frames necessary for the construction of the furniture we manufactured. This company was our major, but not exclusive, supplier of wooden frames, and sharing premises was useful to us both.

Taking the space on Mentana for Jaymar was, for me, like returning home. I had learned the business at that location and most of the employees I had worked with were now working for me, with the important difference that one of my former bosses was now working for me as well.

The building on Mentana had originally belonged to a milk company, J.J. Joubert. The ground floor was a barn where they kept their horses in the days when milk in Montreal was delivered in horse-drawn wagons. There were hooks on the walls of the space and we left them there as a reminder of the city's past and how things change. For some time, we continued to rent the space from the Friedman family, as it owned the building, but after a few years we were able to buy the building outright.

As the business expanded we made changes to the way it was managed. I stopped looking after sales and handed that responsibility over to Nick. I was very bad at sales and every time I got involved in them it ended up costing us money. Either I was too ready to give the retailer a discount on the wholesale price, based on whatever cock-and-bull story he told me, or I would lose my temper and do something to hurt the sale. Nick, on the other hand, was very good at dealing with the retailers who bought our furniture. He enjoyed entertaining the buyers from the department stores, and was good at slipping the sales people a little "something" to promote our product and giving them gift certificates to expensive clothing stores. I wasn't cut out for that kind of work.

I had always been interested in how things were made, so I took responsibility for the manufacturing. I made a point of finding the most efficient way to manufacture our product line while ensuring that the highest quality was maintained. I didn't cut corners. While I was at the orphanage in Budapest I had studied tool making, and I had the necessary knowledge to create the tools we required and design the manufacturing methods we used to improve our products. One example was the way we improved the manufacturing of our sofas, taking the needs of our workers into account. During the process the sofa moved down the production line on a conveyor belt. The original design required workers to bend over to complete their tasks and many of them developed back pains. I designed an improvement to the conveyor belt so that the sofa was moved into a more upright position – that is, standing on its narrow side – so that the workers wouldn't injure their backs.

In addition to improving the manufacturing and design process on the basis of our own ideas and insights, I did my best to learn from other furniture manufacturers that I met. In the 1960s the principal trade show for furniture manufacturers was held at the Chicago Mercantile Mart. In 1965 I attended the trade show as an exhibitor and, as was my habit, I took the time to visit the displays of all the other exhibitors in order to see what I could learn from them. The manufacturer who impressed me the most at that time was an American company called Howard-Parlor. I very much wanted to produce the kind of furniture they made. I met the owner, the son of the founder of the company, Howard Neiderman, and we worked out an arrangement whereby Jaymar would manufacture furniture based on his designs and pay his company a 2 percent royalty.

In addition, I was invited, on many occasions, to visit Howard-Parlor in Chicago to study how they manufactured their furniture. For me, this was like taking a university course in furniture manufacturing. I also learned the techniques that they used for costing the manufacturing process, the kind of machinery they used, and their methods of product development. I put all this information to good use at Jaymar. In order to ensure that our factory instituted and maintained the best practices in the furniture industry, we sent our employees to the Howard-Parlor factory to learn their methods directly.

As a result of our association with Howard-Parlor, Jaymar was able to purchase machinery and raw materials at the same price as they did. On the basis of my commitment to constantly improve our manufacturing process and the quality of our products, Jaymar quickly became an industry leader with an excellent reputation for a well-made, well-designed product that would last a lifetime. We continued our collaboration with Howard-Parlor for the better part of a decade. Our association ended only when Howard Neiderman sold the company.

In the beginning Jaymar worked without a design department. I copied, as best I could, designs from the new model cars. I was an avid reader of trade publications and got ideas from them. I also copied the designs of our competitors. But this could only carry us so far. As our business matured, and thanks to lessons I learned from Howard-Parlor about product development, I decided that Jaymar needed to hire a professional designer. I met Luigi Tiengo, an Italian furniture designer who had been in Canada for just a few years. He worked for several furniture manufacturers. I hired him to work at Jaymar on a royalty basis, paying him a percentage of the sales of the furniture he designed. He would draw a sketch for a new sofa and we would build a model based on that sketch.

I was usually able to work out the cost of manufacturing a sofa product from the sketch, but Jaymar had a sample department where we would construct the new design to be certain we were making the best product in the most efficient way. Sometimes we had to construct and deconstruct the piece to ensure that we were getting the maximum use out of the materials and that labour was being used in the most efficient way possible.

We filmed the way in which the workers built the sofa to see if we could make the operation more efficient for them. Our goal was to reduce the amount of time wasted. We weren't trying simply to speed up the manufacturing process because we knew that would lead to mistakes. Our objective was to improve efficiency. We wanted to make sure that workers didn't have to walk back and forth for their tools, for example. If the tools and the materials were well placed, workers would be able to work more efficiently with less effort. At the end of the process the furniture would be better built and the workers would be less tired.

As we figured out the steps in the manufacturing process we devoted a great deal of time to ensuring that the piece of furniture we were manufacturing was very comfortable. It didn't matter how efficiently we manufactured a sofa if it wasn't comfortable. When customers are in a show room choosing an expensive piece of furniture, its comfort will make or break the sale. As we became more and more experienced at the manufacturing process, we were able to build this comfort into every piece of furniture we made.

Once I worked out the cost of materials and the cost of production I was able to work out the wholesale price. I knew that retailers sold sofas at price points of $499 or $699 or $999, and that to be competitive Jaymar sofas had to be profitable for the retailer at one of those prices. This often meant making design changes in order to reduce the cost of materials, and reducing the time it took to manufacture the product to cut down the cost of labour. We were able to do all of this from a sketch and a model, and we didn't need to bear the expense of having someone draft plans.

I did my best to ensure that Jaymar was among the first to adopt all the improvements that were coming to manufacturing. I wasn't content to adopt only procedures that were invented in Canada and the United States. I travelled to Italy and Germany to see what furniture manufacturers in those countries were doing so that we could compete with any other manufacturer in the world.

In Germany I met with a furniture manufacturer by the name of Rolf Benz. He invited me to visit his factory and this was an educational experience for me. I was greatly impressed with his product line. His furniture was both beautiful and functional. When I told him I thought he made excellent furniture, he replied, "George, it's never good enough!" I was impressed by his attitude and adopted this phrase as my motto. From that point forward my attitude was that, no matter how good our furniture was, it could (and would) always be improved. I was committed to producing a quality product and was certain that, even if I had to charge more in order to produce it, the end-buyer would happily pay more for it.

* * *

When Nick and I started our business I knew a lot about the manufacturing side of things but I knew nothing about the accounting elements that make a business profitable. I recently had a conversation with another businessman who told me that when he started his business he didn't know how to read a balance sheet. When I started my business I had no idea there was such a thing as a balance sheet! And Nick, who had worked as a shipper up until we formed Jaymar, had no better knowledge of how to operate a business.

We made some very costly mistakes in our early days. I had no idea how to do proper cost accounting. When Roger Hébert suggested a price for our product I tended to follow his advice. It took me a while to learn that we were sometimes losing money at his suggested price. As I learned more and more how to evaluate the costs of the component parts of a sofa bed, the cost of everything from thread to staples, from fabric to foam, from the cost of the frame to the cost of its mechanical parts and the cost of labour, I determined to price our product at the right level to cover our costs and turn a profit on each unit. Quality was a more important factor than a low price. I refused to cut corners in order to knock a few dollars off the selling price of a Jaymar product.

We marketed our products to the retail trade more than directly to the consumer. We did buy some billboard advertising but most of our promotion was in trade magazines. It didn't take us long to earn the reputation we were seeking as a manufacturer of a quality product.

In business the temptation is to sell to anyone and everyone. In order not to over-extend ourselves, we had to develop the discipline not to do that. Because of our commitment to quality control, we would get calls from retailers asking if they could carry our furniture. Before committing to signing a sales order I would visit the store to ensure that Jaymar furniture would be well presented in a clean, modern store. There were times when I would visit stores, especially on St Hubert Street, the street in Montreal that became one of the centres of furniture retailing, and tell the owner that I wasn't pleased with the "look" of the store.

I wouldn't allow our products to be placed in a store that had dirty walls and needed a paint job or a store that was too cluttered. This approach seemed obvious to me but apparently it had never been considered before; more than one person thought I was crazy. Retailers felt that if they wanted Jaymar furniture, they should be able to buy it from us and sell it to their customers. They didn't understand why I would give them a hard time. My attitude was that my employees and I had worked hard to make a quality product, and we weren't going to allow it to be sold in an environment that didn't reflect that commitment to quality.

\* \* \*

One of the smartest decisions I made as a young businessman, when I was barely thirty years old in the early 1960s, was to form a business alliance with a man by the name of Neil Genest, who had a sales agency in Quebec City. Genest and his salesmen covered all the towns and villages in the province, the small places that had general stores but no speciality furniture retailers. These stores sold everything, and so did Genest. He was a sales agent for all sorts of products, everything from coffins to kitchen gadgets. He was able to sell Jaymar products to stores in places that none of our other sales reps could get to. We had to sell our furniture to Genest at a big discount so that he could re-sell it at a profit. But he paid us in ten days and this was a big help to our cash flow. We worked with Genest at a time when we couldn't get bank financing, and because he was so prompt in his payments we had the cash on hand to cover our expenses and hold us until our other customers paid.

I enjoyed working with Genest for other reasons as well. He was a highly intelligent man and could have gone far in just about any profession he chose. He did have one problem, though – he was an alcoholic. When he was drunk – and he was drunk a lot of the time – he did crazy things. He was a friend of the then prime minister of Quebec, Jean Lesage. At one point, when he knew that Lesage was flying into the Quebec City airport, Genest hired a plane to fly around the airport and prevent Lesage's plane from landing. I don't know if he thought he was being funny or not, but I do know he was plastered.

When he was in Montreal he stayed at the old Mount Royal Hotel on Peel Street. When he was drunk he would strip off his shirt – not a pretty sight as he was a very fat man – and march around the lobby giving the Nazi salute, shouting Heil Hitler. He was a crazy and obnoxious drunk. But when he was sober I found him to be a sensible and intelligent person who was fascinating to talk to. You just didn't want to be around him when he was drinking.

Happily Genest was smart enough to keep away from me when he was in his cups; I think he sensed that I wouldn't put up with his foolishness and he didn't want to get into a fight with me. I appreciated the fact that he was able to sell our furniture and generate the cash flow we needed to grow our business.

* * *

The road to success for Jaymar was not without its detours – some of which would prove to be costly mistakes.

After the company had been in operation for about seven years, I thought it would be a good idea to get into the business of manufacturing furniture for the office market. In the early 1960s Montreal was gearing up for Expo '67 and office buildings were going up everywhere. In addition, there was talk about a new airport and I thought it would be a good idea to be able to supply it with the institutional-type of furniture it would need. I wanted to manufacture office chairs and waiting room sofas. In 1963 there was a factory on Du Havre Street in the southeastern section of Montreal that was closing. The factory had been in the business of making furniture for restaurants, and it had a complete wood shop, something Jaymar lacked at that time. We signed a three-year lease for the space and intended to use it to manufacture the wood frames we needed for home furniture along with furniture for offices.

Nick and I brought in a third partner by the name of Nat Lazar. He had worked for Samton Metal, a company that made dining room chairs and swivel chairs. Samton Metal had gone out of business. We should have taken that as a sign but we plunged ahead, certain that we could duplicate the success we had in the home furniture business. We called the new product Design Award Chair, obviously hopeful that the name would give us some marketing flair.

Nat knew a lot about the manufacturing side of the metal and swivel chair business but he had no knowledge of how to market the products, and as it turned out neither did we. We thought that if we made a good product we would be able to sell it to commercial customers. We learned the hard way that people who bought office chairs had very specific demands and had designers draw up plans reflecting their ideas. The plans were very difficult to turn into an actual product and we had to make samples for customers' approval. After about five years of trying to break into this business, we decided that we had lost more than enough money and it was time to give up. We did learn a valuable, albeit costly, lesson from our failed entry into the office chair business: stick to what you know – a lesson I repeat to my children and grandchildren.

Actually there was another, greater benefit from our foray into the office chair business. Our apparent mistake actually turned out to have a couple of important advantages. When we rented the space on Du Havre Street, we acquired a wood shop and we hired a fellow named Johnny Schneider to run it. He had worked for a company called Joel and had managed its wood shop. Schneider was a very practical and well-organized man with a lot of common sense and he did a great job of running the wood shop. He was also an excellent manager, and with him on board we became entirely self-sufficient. We could now manufacture the wood frames we needed for our furniture. I would rather have acquired these benefits in a less costly way but I was happy with the results.

There was to be one more lucky fork on the road to success that occurred later as we were in the process of closing the shop on Du Havre and solving the problem of how to bring the manufacture of the frames in-house.

As Jaymar grew so did our need for manufacturing space. By the mid-1960s we outgrew the building we owned on Mentana. We purchased one hundred thousand square feet of land on Langelier Boulevard in Saint Léonard, a suburb east of Montreal. Our plan was to build a larger factory there. But, as happened on many occasions in my life, a chance encounter brought us another opportunity.

One Sunday, when I was out for a drive with Eleanor and our daughters, we stopped at a chip wagon in the town of Terrebonne, about twenty-five kilometres from Montreal. While we were there eating food that was probably unhealthy but too delicious to resist, a man approached me. "I know you," he said. "You're a wrestler." His name was Sam Butler. I introduced him to my family and we had a nice relaxed chat – as is common when you run into people in the country.

Typically, when two businessmen meet, even on a Sunday at a chip wagon, the conversation turns to business. Sam told me he owned a lot of land in the region, in the town of Terrebonne. He described the area as an up-and-coming region with two new highways and a bridge (a necessity as Montreal is an island) soon to be built. I told him that Jaymar had just bought land in Saint Léonard but that we had discovered that we had to be on a railroad siding in order to ship our furniture to our customers in the western provinces.

Sam told me that there was a lot of available land next to railroad sidings in Terrebonne and that the two modern highways to be built in the area would give easy access to the region. He told us he would be pleased to introduce me to the mayor of the town, Claude Paquette.

Sam took us to meet Mayor Paquette and we spent a very nice afternoon with him. He had three daughters about the same ages as our girls and the six of them played while the adults talked. Mayor Paquette is a lawyer who lived (and still lives) in Terrebonne but had his law office in Montreal. He was very keen to have Jaymar locate in his town and offered to do anything he could to help us build a factory there. He wanted to establish the industrial base of the region, and Jaymar was exactly the kind of

company he thought of as ideal for Terrebonne. I liked the area
and I especially liked the way in which Mayor Paquette made me
feel welcome, so we bought some land next to a railway siding
in Terrebonne.

While we were working out the deal to buy the Terrebonne
land, we had to do something about the land we had purchased in
Saint Léonard. Clearly it had to be sold. Jaymar didn't have
enough money to own two parcels of land. Luckily for us the value
of the land in Saint Leonard had gone up during the time we
owned it and we were able to sell it at enough of a profit to cover
the cost of building part of our factory in Terrebonne.

We started small in Terrebonne. At first we only built a wood
shop of about 25,000 square feet to make the frames for the sofas.
The upholstering was still done in Montreal. This meant that we
shipped the wood frames back to Montreal so that the manufacturing process could be completed and then we shipped the finished products back to Terrebonne, where we were on a railroad
siding, to be shipped to the retailer.

But Jaymar continued to grow, and by 1972 we had enough
money to build additional factory space in Terrebonne and we
moved the entire operation there. And we still retained ownership
of the building on Mentana.

* * *

The government of Quebec played an important role in helping
the furniture industry in the province to stay abreast of innova-
tions in the industry. Along with forming the trade association,
L'Association des Fabricants de Meubles du Québec, it organized
trade missions for members to travel to Europe to learn from manufacturers there. The largest trade show in the furniture business is
held in Cologne, Germany, and government-sponsored trips were
arranged to coincide with that event.

I had mixed emotions when I first considered participating in
one of these fact-finding missions. I harboured a lot of negative
feelings toward Germany and Germans owing to the suffering
they caused to European Jewry and my family in particular. These
feelings were at their strongest when I was a young man, newly

arrived in Canada. Over time, and once I had the opportunity to meet German émigrés to Canada, these feelings abated somewhat. (We had neighbours in the Laurentians, a couple, Walter and Brigitte, who were from Germany. They were very nice people, good neighbours, and good friends.)

The engineer who designed the mechanism for our first line of Make-A-Bed products was originally from Germany. So when I had the chance to join with other Quebec furniture manufacturers to take in the trade show in Cologne and visit factories in Germany, I decided to take advantage of the opportunity. I had two main reasons for becoming part of the group. The first and most obvious was to see what was going on in Europe in general and in Germany in particular and to learn from what I observed. The second reason was so that I could make myself put the past, not behind me – I wasn't ready for that – but to the side.

It became my habit when travelling to Germany to take a few extra days and go skiing in Switzerland. On one of my ski trips I met a group of young Germans who told me that they had been to Israel and that they intended to return there so they could work on a kibbutz. Little by little, as time went by, I began to understand that the German people were trying to come to terms with their past, to admit that they had done a serious wrong, and to move forward by making reparations for the past and ensuring that such a thing could never happen again.

I couldn't say as much for other European countries, especially Hungary. The Hungarians had never admitted their guilt and the country had not made any effort to make amends for its past behaviour.

I must say that the more often I travelled to Germany the more I enjoyed it. There were added benefits to travelling with my colleagues from Quebec. I got to know them and they got to know me, and we developed strong business and personal ties. As I was the only member of the group who could speak German, I was an invaluable and popular member of our group.

In the early 1970s, following the trade show in Cologne, I was flying to Switzerland for a couple of days of skiing, and I was seated next to a man who introduced himself as Bob. He worked for *Der Speigel*, one of the leading magazines in Germany, and he told me that he was with a group of friends who were heading to St Moritz for the skiing. In the course of our conversation he invited me to join them. I had no specific plans and was delighted with the invitation. Included in the group was a woman by the name of Mrs Rodenstock, whose husband was the largest manufacturer of lenses for eyeglasses and for cameras manufactured by the Leica Company.

I later learned that the Leica Company had saved the lives of many thousands of Jews in the years before the Holocaust. The wife of the ex-Shah of Iran was also part of their group. I have to admit that they were a class of people with whom I had had very little contact in my life, but I found them to be very welcoming and generous and not arrogant in any way. Most of the German people didn't want to discuss the past or even the politics of the present. From time to time I would bring up past events but I couldn't get my German friends to discuss them. They said they wanted to live in the present and leave politics to the politicians.

At first I was a little taken aback when they told me that the plan was to meet to start skiing at noon. I was used to getting an early start on the hills. As it turned out my new friends attended dinners and parties in the evening, events that could continue into the wee hours of the morning, and they liked to sleep in. They included me in their evening activities, and so I adopted their habit of getting a late start to the day. The time I spent with my new friends was always happy and fun-filled.

On another of my visits to Germany I made a side trip to Munich to visit Mr and Mrs Rodenstock. They had a very elegant and affluent lifestyle but they weren't the kind of people to show off their wealth. Mr Rodenstock impressed me with his business acumen. At one point, while explaining his business philosophy, he said, "You know, George, you must charge as much as you can, when you can. In business you never know what the future is." I took his advice to heart.

The Rodenstocks made me feel at home and they took the trouble to show me around the city of Munich. I wanted to see the site of the Olympics that had been held there the previous summer. As a Jew and an athlete I was very much moved by the massacre that had occurred and wanted to pay my respects at the site of the tragedy. The Rodenstocks made the visit with me and I sensed that they too were upset by the events.

On one of my trips to Switzerland I met some Japanese skiers. I was impressed by the quality of their ski clothing and equipment and I complimented them on it. In the course of our chat they discovered that I was from Canada. They told me that they believed that the clothing and equipment made in Canada wasn't of as high a quality as that made in Japan. The Germans made the same observation. From these conversations I learned that no matter how good I thought Jaymar furniture to be, it was not good enough. This became my credo: we would always try to make our furniture better.

With this credo in mind, I took our designer, Luigi Tiengo, with me on one of my trips to Europe so that he could see what was taking place in our industry there. I wanted him to get a sense of current European designs so that he could adapt them to Jaymar's furniture for the American and Canadian markets. I made many contacts in the furniture industry in Europe and learned a great deal about their manufacturing processes from them. I was keen to produce furniture designed with a European influence.

When I got back to Montreal I pushed my partner and my staff to work hard to improve our furniture. We had to find ways to make it better today than we made it yesterday and to make it better again tomorrow. This attitude tended to drive the people around me crazy but it did result in a better product. And I owe the success of Jaymar to the high quality of its products.

In addition to making friends with many furniture manufacturers and equipment suppliers in Germany, I also visited Italy. Leather furniture became popular in Europe in the late 1970s, and we added it to Jaymar's product line. I bought leather from an Italian company, Compel, owned by a man named Sergio Monserati. He and his secretary, Rosy, became very good friends of Eleanor's and mine. Sergio had a sybaritic lifestyle and this, I fear, led to his early death. We are still very good friends with Rosy and we see her and her husband, Giuseppe, whenever we can.

In order to better communicate with my friends in Italy, especially with Sergio and Rosy, I decided to learn Italian. I asked my barber, who was Italian, to recommend someone to act as my tutor and he put me in touch with a friend of his, a tailor, who worked with me to master what I consider to be the most beautiful language in the world. It is true that I speak Italian with a Hungarian accent, but I have no trouble making myself understood in that language and I read it without difficulty.

The fact that I made regular trips to Europe had an unexpected and unanticipated effect on my family life. When Eleanor and I got married we lived on Dupuis Street near the corner of Legaré, not far from where her parents lived. In 1960, after the birth of our daughter Marla, we moved to Chomedey, a northern suburb on Montreal. Our second and third daughters, Aviva and Judith, were born while we lived there. Chomedey was nice enough but my travels to Europe instilled in me the desire to live a more sophisticated urban life. I found the suburb where we lived to be uninspiring. While we were living there our house was robbed and this made the area even less attractive to Eleanor.

In 1972 we moved back into the city, where we rented an apartment on Bonavista Avenue on the west side of Mount Royal close to Westmount, the area where some of Montreal's richest people live. I enjoyed the proximity to downtown but the children missed the suburb where they could play outside with their friends. In 1975 we built our own home in the wealthy, west-end suburb of Hampstead, which was not too far from Montreal's city centre, and where our girls could safely play outdoors.

* * *

During the time that I travelled to Europe and started construction of the family home in Hampstead, Auntie Annie was a constant part of our life. She treated me like a son and our children as if they were her grandchildren. She babysat for us when we went out for the evening or went on vacation. In the same way that she treated me like her son, she considered Eleanor to be her daughter-in-law. Not surprisingly, given the strong characters of the two women, some friction developed between them. Eleanor is not the type of person to sidestep a problem and she made it clear to Auntie that she had to respect her role as wife and mother and not interfere. Auntie only wanted the best for all of us and accommodated my wife.

Auntie worked in the accounting department at Jaymar virtually from its inception. When we moved to Terrebonne she moved with us. I would drive her to work and home every day. One day, as I was returning from lunch I came across a couple of well-dressed businessmen entering our office. I knew just about everybody in the area and I certainly knew our suppliers and customers but I didn't know these two fellows. I overheard them ask the receptionist if they could see Mrs Pugatch. This surprised me as I couldn't imagine what contact Auntie Annie could have had with these two men, who were clearly strangers.

They introduced themselves, telling me they were from Union Carbide, an international chemical company that supplied us with plastic products, and that they had received a letter from Mrs Pugatch that they wanted to discuss with her. This only added to the mystery, rather than solving it. I asked them what the letter was about – my first thought was that Auntie may have sent them a letter attacking the company politically.

As it turned out, Auntie Annie had noticed that they were undercharging us for the products they sold to us and wrote to tell them that if they were not more careful in their business practices they would soon be out of business. These two representatives of Union Carbide had come to our factory in Terrebonne to meet Auntie and thank her personally for her honesty. The two football-player-size executives offering humble thanks to Auntie, who was less than five feet tall, made for an amusing scene; a memory that I find droll to this day. I was very pleased for Annie and very proud of her.

The 1970s were a period of growth for Jaymar furniture, and our corporate culture was exemplified by Auntie's attitude toward Union Carbide. We were successful because we built a reputation for having a quality product and we treated our suppliers and our customers with honesty and respect. Some of our customers made errors in pricing their orders to us – at times these errors were in our favour. In each and every case we called the customer and told them to resubmit the order at the correct price, which had the effect of increasing the customer's profit margin. This attitude strengthened our relations with our customers and ensured that we received a lot of repeat business from that customer.

* * *

Late in the year, in December 1974, tragedy again came into my life. My beloved Auntie Annie passed away. At the age of eighty she caught a cold that lingered and then turned into pneumonia. I was in touch with Auntie on a daily basis and often more than once a day. When I discovered that her cold wasn't getting better, I insisted that we go to the hospital. It was there that she was diagnosed with life-threatening pneumonia. The doctors did everything they could to cure Auntie and save her life, but in the end she made her own decision. She told me that at the age of eighty she was very tired and that I had to let her go. This incredible woman to whom I owed so much wanted to say good-bye and thank me for being part of her life.

Auntie Annie was everything to me: mother, advisor, friend, and companion. She played a significant role in my life from the moment I met her. Her influence continued long after her death, right up to the present. She taught me one of the most important and hardest lessons I had to learn as I began my new life in Canada – she helped me to understand that in order to deal with my past and have a happy life it was necessary to forgive past events without forgetting them. Frankly, this was an extremely hard thing for me to do and I doubt that I could have done it without Auntie's support and encouragement in all things.

She loved me unconditionally and I felt the same way about her. Everyone at Jaymar was touched by Auntie's kindness and helpfulness, and like me they were devastated at her passing. We were all richer for having known her.

* * *

As the business grew, my relationship with Nick also changed. When we started out, we had to work closely together to make Jaymar successful. As time went on, however, we grew apart. There were two major reasons for this. The first and the most understandable is that we were both married and our social lives centred on our families rather than each other. In the early days of the company, Nick and I worked together and we tended to socialize as well. This is easy to do when you are single and working long hours; harder when spending time with your family as well.

Another developing fissure in our relationship had to do with our managerial styles. I was very hands-on. I needed to understand how every aspect of the business worked and how all the parts came together to form a whole. Because of my experience and knowledge of manufacturing, I knew in detail how a piece of furniture was made and if a problem arose I was more than capable of solving it. I could determine the cost price of a piece of Jaymar furniture with ease, and priced our product according to the real cost of production and in concert with the pricing philosophy I learned from Mr Rodenstock on my visit to Munich. Nick, on the other hand, had a less detailed knowledge of the business in that he concentrated on sales and administration.

More important, I was committed to always acquiring the most modern, best equipment available for our factory. This sometimes required a capital outlay. But the return was always greater than the cost of equipment. Nick was less willing to spend money while we had machinery that he considered "good enough." My philosophy was that it was "never good enough." And this in a nutshell is where Nick and I mostly disagreed. Our differences would soon have to be resolved.

\* \* \*

During the period that I was growing my business I discovered that my family was, in fact, one person larger than I had thought. Lazar Rothschild, Rothschild Bácsi, the man who became a second father to me, the man who saved so many Jewish lives in Hungary during the Nazi occupation, and the man who was responsible for my immigrating to Canada, had a surprise for me.

Uncle Rothschild, as I called him, had after the war been imprisoned in Hungary for his life-saving activities during the war. During the Hungarian Revolution of 1956 he was freed and he made his way to Canada. Once here he became a part of the Hungarian community of Jewish expatriates who in one way or another survived the war. We considered ourselves to be an extended family

In the mid-1970s we were at a wedding of the daughter of a member of this extended family. Uncle Rothschild told me he had a story to tell me but was reluctant to do so. This struck me as an odd way to introduce the topic. Either he had something to tell me or he didn't; and if he didn't want to tell me what was on his mind why bring it up at all? It was clear that he had something momentous to say and it was just as clear that he didn't know how to broach the subject. After all we had been through, I couldn't imagine what it was that was preying on his mind. After a little more hemming and hawing he blurted out the thing that he had been holding back from me.

"You have a half-brother in Hungary," he said.

If I had been asked to make a list of all the possible surprising things that Uncle Rothschild had to tell me, this would not have been on the list! But once he had told me this surprising news, it took very little further prompting to get him to tell me the rest of the story.

Uncle Rothschild would, from time to time, visit my hometown of Szikszó, in order to visit the cemetery to pay his respects to his dead parents. He would fly to Budapest and from there take the train to Miskolc, the second-largest city in Hungary. He would make the last leg of his journey, from Miskolc to Szikszó, a distance of some seventeen kilometres by taxi. On one of his journeys he and the taxi driver fell into a conversation about Szikszó and its past. It was obvious to the taxi driver that Uncle Rothschild, because he was visiting the Jewish cemetery, had been a resident of the town before the war. The cabbie asked Uncle Rothschild if he knew what had happened to Jacob Reinitz, my father. Uncle Rothschild asked him why he was interested in Jacob Reinitz and the driver responded, "Because he was my father." Uncle Rothschild could scarcely believe his ears. He told the driver that my father had died on the Death March but that Jacob had a son, George, who had survived the war.

The cabbie's mother, a Christian woman, had been a domestic servant in my grandfather's house in Hegymeg. When my father was eighteen, he had a relationship with her and got her pregnant.

The domestic ultimately left Hegymeg and moved to Miskolc, had her baby, and later got married.

When I learned that I had a half-brother, I of course wanted to find him, and I made a trip to Miskolc to search for him. I asked every cab driver I could find in that city if he knew a cabbie with the name of Reinitz. I even tried to get in touch with any family I could find with the name Reinitz, even though they were not related to me. (Many of these Reinitzes that I found wanted to adopt me into their families even though we were not related. I guess they wanted to have a relative living in Canada.)

Finally, I went back to the town of Hegymeg, where my father had lived before moving to Szikszó and where my half-brother's mother had worked for my grandparents. I found the town crier of Hegymeg, Mr Toth,* a very old man by this time. He confirmed the story for me and told me that he remembered my father's other son. They were friends and they would go to my grandmother's store and she would give them candy. Mr Toth was a wonderful old man and he was able to tell me what had happened to my half-brother. As it turned out, he didn't go by the name of Reinitz but had taken the name of his mother's husband.

I made a second trip to Hungary to find him and was able to locate his family in Miskolc. That is, I found the house that Mr Toth directed me to but discovered that he had moved. I then found the house he had moved to, where his family lived, but arrived just too late to meet my half-brother. He had died about three months before I got there. I did get the opportunity to meet his wife, though, and his daughter and his grandson. His wife knew the true story of her husband's father, but his children and grandchildren did not. They were as surprised as I had been when they learned of his lineage.

As it turned out, my half-brother's friends used to tease him and gave him the nickname, the Jew. His wife thought they called him that because he was always negotiating. Frankly, this doesn't seem like unusual behaviour for a taxi driver! Perhaps they gave him that nickname because he looked Jewish – I saw a picture of him and

---

* Coincidentally the town crier bore the same name but was not related to the fellow that Mr Rothschild wanted me to try to find in Canada.

there was a strong resemblance to my father and therefore to me. In any event, it does not appear that his friends meant the nickname as a compliment – although he may have taken it as one.

On my final trip to Hungary in 2004 with my grandchildren Brett and Amara, I went to see Mr Toth for what turned out to be the last time. He was very ill and could barely speak but I did have the opportunity to say good-bye to a man I considered to be very kind and possessed of a natural intelligence, a man I had come to like very much.

# 8

# Jaymar, 1980–2000

Nick and I had come a long way since we started our business in July of 1956 but by 1980 I had no choice: the differences that had emerged between us absolutely had to be resolved.

When Nick and I set up business together, neither of us knew much about how to structure a company, or how to set up audit and management controls so that each of us could have easy access to the information we needed to ascertain the health of our business. Both of us had signing privileges on our bank account and so neither of us had to inform the other before writing cheques. I know better than to allow this kind of situation now, but at the time, in 1956, things like this didn't seem important. One of the disputes that arose between Nick and me had to do with cash disbursements and revolved around the fact that he made certain expenditures about which I was unaware.

But this was not the most serious problem that developed between us. More serious was the difference in our management styles. As things evolved at Jaymar, as I have mentioned, I took care of design and production and Nick looked after sales and administration. Part of his job was to make sure that the employees in the office were happy at their jobs and that any conflicts were resolved in a fair way. In my opinion, Nick was not successful at handling these kinds of responsibilities. For instance, when an employee would ask for a raise Nick would negotiate hard, putting the employee in a difficult situation. An employer might not be able to give an employee a raise but he should never demoralize the employee by being overly aggressive. When Nick and the employee finally agreed on an amount, Nick would sometimes forget to process the pay increase and the employee would have to remind him of their agreement. Sometimes it would take an employee three weeks to get the promised raise.

This type of thing led to unnecessary conflicts that were difficult to settle and created a mood of tension and mistrust in the office. This disturbed me because it was not my way of doing things. It is only natural that if employees can't trust their employers to honour their commitments they will not do their best for the company; they will not feel like they are valuable members of a team.

My business philosophy, if you can call it that, came from the time I worked with my father. I learned from him that if you give people a little more than they expect they will feel good about themselves and put out the extra effort that makes a business successful. As far as I was concerned, once the company reached an agreement with an employee it was important to honour it as quickly as possible. In the case of a salary increase I felt that the employee had a right to receive it on his or her next pay. I never forgot the feeling of being an employee. I remembered how unappreciated I felt when I approached my bosses at Montreal Upholstering to ask for the right to purchase some equity in the firm. I could sort of understand why the Friedmans might not want to have a non-family member in the firm; but I also remembered how hurt I was that they didn't recognize my contribution to their company. When it came my turn, I wanted Jaymar's employees to feel valued.

I also had the example of my father. He knew that it was important to treat his workers fairly and not to ask them to do things in a way that could cause them injury. He was always very quick to work with them to ensure that the work he expected of them was fair. Because his employees knew that my father would, when necessary, provide extra for them, they gave a little extra effort for him.

Nick had a very different background than I did, in that his father was a lawyer. He never had the chance to learn how to work with employees, to understand how important it was to motivate them.

I shouldn't be too harsh about Nick's failure to treat the employees well in that, in the early 1970s while we were operating in two locations, Jaymar was unionized by the Teamsters. I always did my best to treat our employees with respect, to help them when needed. At times when employees needed a loan or some other form of assistance it was my policy to help them out as best I could. I did this because I understood too well what it was like to need money and not have access to it, especially when you have to take care of a family. And I have to say that when I made a loan to an employee I was always paid back in full, unless, of course it was a forgivable loan. When the balance owing was small or if I knew that an employee was having difficulties or family problems, I would arrange to forget about the amount I was owed. I have to say that the employees never took advantage of me and loans were forgiven at my suggestion not theirs. I believed that employees were people not spreadsheets.

Because I was busy supervising the construction of the factory in Terrebonne, I hired a foreman to look after production. Unfortunately, this foreman was not as considerate of the employees as I had been. He was very tough. If an employee had a problem with punctuality, he would not work with the employee to help him to understand the importance of being on time. He would not treat the tardiness as a problem to be solved. Instead he would punish the employee by sending him or her home. More often than not the employee had a good reason for being late, perhaps that one of his kids was sick. It is fairly easy to solve a problem of this nature by ensuring that the employee has an opportunity to communicate the fact that he would be late and the reason for it. The foreman's attitude caused a lot of bad feeling and this led to the employees forming a union. I blame myself for not hiring the right person to act as foreman and for not making sure he understood my management philosophy.

All in all, we learned to live with the union. Things were a little more stressful when the president of the union at Jaymar – her name was Suzanne – insisted that she have a private office and be allowed, at full pay, to be able to devote as much time as she believed necessary to union business. This was a bitter pill to swallow. On the other hand, I must have been doing something right because at the company Christmas party Suzanne insisted on dancing with me. So, overall, other than a short strike in the

summer of 1978, our relations with our employees were good –
better than in many other businesses.

As a result of the formation of the union, we established a professional Human Resources Department. Monique Bastien, the
head of our HR department, was a very intelligent and experienced
executive, and she installed procedures that improved the morale of
the workers. She initiated a newsletter that went to all our employees. It provided news about the company and special events in the
lives of the employees, and we also used it to compliment employees who did an exceptional job or were able to improve the way we
operated. The production employees still had to pay a portion of
their wages to the union, and Suzanne, as president, was more interested in protecting the union than solving the problems of individual employees. But Monique did take an interest in each of the
employees, and did her best to ensure that policies were fair and
fairly applied.

And this brings me back to one of the differences I had with
Nick. When I discovered a problem with the employees in the factory I did my best to resolve it to our mutual benefit – even in a
situation where the union was involved. The problems Nick had in
the administration side of the business were never resolved.

More fundamentally, I was hurt by something that Nick did. My
view of a partnership involved a sharing of everything. If one of
the partners did something for his own benefit he had a moral
obligation to let his partner benefit equally – even if the benefit
arose from an opportunity that had nothing to do with Jaymar. I
discovered that Nick had made some investments that did very
well. I knew that if I had had the information that Nick had, I
would have shared it with him so that we both could have benefited. He didn't do this. I found this hurtful and I felt that this was
the wrong way to behave.

Additional issues came between us as well. I wanted to have the
latest equipment and to produce furniture of the highest quality
so that we would have a substantial business that would last well
into the future, a heritage business that could be taken over by our
children. Nick was more interested in short-term gain. And finally
there was the fact that we had grown apart socially. In the early
days of Jaymar we worked together and spent some of our free

time together. However, the fact that we spent less and less time in one another's company outside of work after we married had a negative effect on our relationship at the factory. In the period leading up to the dissolution of our partnership I actually felt, for the first time since we started the company, that my heart was not in Jaymar. It came to the point that I didn't look forward to going to work. This was a terrible feeling, and I knew I had to find a way to change it.

I felt awful that we could no longer work together but I felt that I had no option but to come to some kind of an arrangement with Nick to end our business partnership. I made an offer to Nick that I believed was fair and just. I offered to buy out his share of the business for a seven-figure amount, or he could buy me out at the same evaluation. I anticipated that he would want the buyout as I believed that he wouldn't be able to run the company without me. I arranged for financing and the bank did its due-diligence investigation of our business and agreed to lend me the money I needed.

Nick, for his part, wanted time to determine his options. He was a smart man and he knew that if he bought me out I would open another furniture factory and he would have to compete with me. He was also justifiably worried that many of the employees would want to work with me and he would lose them. So in the end he made the rational decision to accept a buyout. I gave him as much cash as I could plus the building on Mentana Street, which was fully rented. On top of this I owed him an additional amount as a balance of the sale.

\* \* \*

There remained one further issue to resolve when we broke up our partnership. We had, with a third partner and a relative of mine, formed a company that supplied small upholstering companies with textiles.

Jaymar purchased textiles for its furniture from various suppliers. In the mid-1970s a sales representative from one of these suppliers, Bernie Ovenson, came to me with a business proposition. His plan, based on his knowledge of the market, was a straightforward one. He noticed that there were a lot of small companies that did furniture re-upholstering in Montreal that had trouble getting the textiles they needed in small quantities and in a timely fashion. Ovenson, who was from Toronto, knew that he could acquire a variety of textiles in small quantities from suppliers who had product left over from their large customers. These textile manufacturers didn't know who the small Montreal re-upholstering companies were and so had no way of supplying them.

Ovenson's simple idea was to get orders from the small companies and have the textiles shipped to them overnight from Toronto. This would solve a number of problems. First, the re-upholsterers would not have to carry inventory, a drain on their cash flow. They could order only what they needed to meet their demands. And best of all, the business that handled these transactions would be profitable, as it didn't have to own the product it was selling. I talked to Nick about this idea and he was in favour of it, so we partnered with Bernie Ovenson and set up a company we called Joann Fabrics.

There was an added benefit to having this company. I had a second cousin, John Benedict, who lived in Israel, where he worked as a taxi driver. Just before we started Joann Fabrics I was able to sponsor him to come to Canada and he worked at Jaymar. I was thrilled to have a family member back in my life, living in Montreal. John and his wife, Miriam, and Eleanor and I would socialize a lot. This relationship gave me great pleasure, as it was the first time since I left Hungary all those years ago that I had a family member close at hand. John's wife and Eleanor formed a very strong friendship.

John was an affable fellow. His fellow employees at Jaymar liked him almost as much as I did. He was great fun to be around and had wonderful social skills. It didn't take him long to adjust to his new life in Canada.

Because of my strong connection to my cousin I wanted to help him in any way that I could and so I set him up in a business: Benedict Textiles. John's company would, in effect, act as the sales arm of Joann Fabrics, selling textiles to small re-upholstering companies in Quebec. The plan was that this company would buy fabric from Joann Fabrics at 10 percent above its cost. Benedict would buy the fabric he needed, on the basis of his orders, and thus didn't have to carry any inventory. Joann Fabrics shipped his orders to him overnight and he delivered them to his customers. I was pleased to be able to set him up in his own company as I wanted him to have a secure future. He had a rent-free office in our building on Mentana. As an added benefit, I sold him any textiles that I could from Jaymar's supplies. I sold him these textiles at Jaymar's cost. Jaymar did not make any money on these sales but it meant that my cousin's company would be profitable.

Joann Fabrics was a successful company and things were going well for all of us until Nick and I broke up our partnership in Jaymar. Clearly, Nick harboured some very bad feelings: he got together with Bernie Ovenson and they decided to force me out of the business. They couldn't force me to sell my equity in Joann Fabrics, but they could harm Benedict's business by not honouring his purchase orders. Nick and Bernie knew that I wouldn't abandon my cousin and that their plan would make me want to sell out. If Benedict could not fulfill his orders he was essentially out of business. I thought that this kind of emotional blackmail was an underhanded way of forcing me out of the business Nick and I owned with Ovenson, but there was little I could do about it.

As I mentioned earlier, I owed Nick an amount of money as a balance of sale for his share of Jaymar. I offered to sell him my equity in Joann Fabrics for the amount I owed him which would wipe out my debt to him. Nick accepted my offer. But as a result of this transfer of equity, John Benedict had to close his company as he could no long depend on Joann Fabrics to act as a supplier. These events put the finishing touches on my partnership (and my friendship) with Nick. I had no idea how he and Bernie arranged their business partnership after I left Joann Fabrics. My suspicion is that Bernie somehow came out ahead in their relationship.

This setback did not mean that I would give up trying to help my cousin or the business of supplying re-upholsterers. Jaymar was a large customer for textiles and we could easily supply the re-upholsterers from our inventory. We also had the buying power to purchase supplies for that market. I set up a company called Redecor Fabrics with my cousin. John did not invest as much money as I did, but he was able to make a contribution to the company, which I appreciated. I provided most of the capital for the business and I had the ability to arrange for a line of credit from the bank so that I owned 51 percent of the equity. It was critical that I remain the majority shareholder as I was personally liable for any debt owing the bank and I had to have the ability to make the important decisions if for some reason I didn't like the direction the company was taking.

In the beginning Redecor Fabrics was doing a decent business. I hoped that it would grow and prosper and in its early days my son-in-law Perry Birman was also a partner in Redecor Fabrics. He remained in the company until he and my daughter, Marla, relocated to Florida. The business produced a small profit – enough to support its principals but not much more than that.

Before long, problems started to develop. My cousin John, who on a personal level was a wonderful fellow, was not an easy person to work with. He opposed just about every idea that came his way. When I wanted to purchase computers to automate inventory management, he claimed that computers were not good, that the business did not need them. This, of course, made no sense and after a time I got tired of fighting with him about everything. One of his unusual ideas was that we should increase our prices in order to increase our profit margin. It didn't seem to occur to him that an increase in prices would cause a decrease in sales and thus reduce our profitability. It would have been smarter by far to increase volume.

I had set up the business to help my cousin and my son-in-law Perry. I didn't draw a salary or any other benefit from Redecor Fabrics, even though I owned 51 percent of it. I helped my cousin and son-in-law wherever and whenever I could; but I didn't want Redecor Fabrics to be a drain on my time and energy.

One beautiful Saturday morning I went into the office to have it out with Benedict. I told him that I wanted to install computers to make the management of the business more efficient. He insisted, ridiculously, that computers were neither good nor necessary. Finally, I told him that I was tired of wasting time fighting with him. "It's a beautiful day," I said. "I could be out playing golf but instead I am here arguing with you. I don't want to live with you anymore. I tried to help you but you are not interested, so you are out." I paid my cousin back the full amount of his investment in the company, which meant that he would be able to start another business and that he didn't have to cover any of the losses, including a large bank loan, that Redecor had incurred. This was a very generous act on my part, as the company was losing half a million dollars at that time. And that was that, as far as our business relationship was concerned.

It was a lot more difficult to lose contact with my cousin on a personal level, which is what happened when our business connection ended. I had very few relatives left after the war and those I did have were precious to me. I had been pleased to be able to bring John and his family to Canada, so it saddened me a great deal that we didn't remain close. Eleanor also felt the loss of her close friend, John's wife, Miriam.

The loss of her friendship with Miriam was doubly hard on Eleanor, as she had advised me not to set John up in business in the first place. She was concerned that if things didn't go well we would lose two close friends and relatives. She was right and I wish I had listened to her.

I kept Redecor Fabrics running for a couple of years in order to try to mitigate my losses in the company but in the end I closed it as it was not a viable business.

\* \* \*

Following the buyout, Nick tried his hand at a couple of different businesses. He first went into the construction business with a friend of his. Then, after a while he went back into the furniture business with a competitor of Jaymar. But this factory made low-end furniture and Nick's involvement with the company lasted only a short time. He saw that competing with Jaymar was impossible. Jaymar was not interested in the low end of the market and it was difficult to compete with us at the high end.

At first I missed Nick. We had been together a long time and had been through a lot since we met on the train heading from Budapest to Paris in 1948. I missed the camaraderie of our partnership. But as time went on, I had to admit that I enjoyed having the freedom to make all the decisions regarding the business without having lengthy discussions with a partner. On the other hand I recognized the importance of discussing operational issues, and so I organized a team of key employees from various parts of the company. We discussed any problems that arose and made decisions on how best to solve them. This form of management worked out much better than having to convince a partner to do something that was clearly in the interest of the company. And I was able to buy the modern equipment from Europe that I wanted.

But there were moments when I feared that I might have made a serious mistake. Very soon after I bought Nick out in 1980 there was a stock market crash, interest rates soared to 20 percent and higher, and all businesses, Jaymar included, suffered. In order to ensure the survival of Jaymar, I lowered my salary. We cut expenses everywhere we could and made ourselves more efficient. At no point did we ask the employees to take a reduction in salary; I felt that burden belonged to me alone.

The eight years following buying out Nick were tough from a business standpoint but apart from momentary worries I never doubted that I had done the right thing.

\* \* \*

Over the years Jaymar became a major player in the Canadian market. The company had a permanent showroom at the Canadian Home Furniture Association building in Ontario, and Jaymar participated in the annual trade show in Toronto. I also wanted to improve our sales in the United States.

The best, the most efficient, and the most profitable way to sell into the American market was to have a showroom at the American Home Furnishings Alliance complex in High Point, North Carolina. This group held two trade shows each year and, like all trade shows in all industries, it was important for manufacturers to exhibit at the trade shows so that retail customers could see the new designs and products and place their orders.

It was critically important to have a permanent showroom at the American Home Furnishings Alliance campus. The world's major furniture manufacturers from around the world had showrooms in High Point. In order to be considered a major player in the industry, it was necessary to have a permanent showroom there. Even after thirty years in the business, Jaymar was unsuccessful in being able to rent showroom space in High Point. The man in charge of showroom rentals was a gentleman by the name of Mr de Luca. I did my best to arrange an appointment with him, but even that was impossible. I telephoned him frequently to that end. He was well aware that there was more demand for showroom space than there was space available; he knew I was calling to try to persuade him to rent space to my company and he avoided my calls.

I am not the type of person to give up when there is something I want. I learned in Auschwitz that if I wanted extra food for my father and myself I would have to jump the fence to the kitchen area to retrieve the potato skins that the prisoners who peeled the potatoes left in the yard. If I was prepared to risk my life for potato skins, I was not about to be deterred by Mr de Luca's refusal to meet with me. I was determined to see him. When I was in High Point for the trade show, instead of making another phone call that he would ignore, I went directly to his office. I presented myself at the reception desk and asked to see Mr de Luca. The receptionist announced over the public address system that there was a Mr Reinitz in the reception area to see Mr de Luca. I was so anxious to see him that I didn't even sit down. I remained standing so that when he came into the reception area we would be able to start a conversation face to face.

As I was waiting I suddenly felt someone grab me from behind. It would be an understatement to say that I was surprised. I wondered if I had done something very wrong by trying to approach Mr de Luca without an appointment and was being thrown out of the office by security. The person who had me in a very tight grip said, "I know Reinitz. There is only one Reinitz, George Reinitz." I recognized the voice immediately and I turned around to find Bruce Miller, a friend I hadn't seen in twenty years. I had no idea what Bruce was doing there. I had taught him wrestling at the Montreal Y. We were thrilled to see one another and continued to wrestle. When Mr de Luca came into the reception area he found two grown men in business suits wrestling like adolescents, each trying to take the other down. He must have thought we were crazy – or worse, that one of us was trying to attack the other.

In the midst of much laughter, Bruce and I stopped our wrestling to talk to Mr de Luca. It turned out that Bruce Miller was his boss, the president of the American Home Furnishings Alliance. Once we regained our composure and expressed our joy at seeing one another after so long a time, Bruce made it clear to his showroom agent that Jaymar was to be treated with kid gloves. He didn't care how it was done, but we were to be given the best showroom space possible. "I don't care if you have to move people," Bruce told Mr de Luca, "Give Mr Reinitz whatever he wants." And that is how we managed to get showroom space at the most important furniture organization in North America.

Bruce went beyond arranging for us to have showroom space. He also fixed up the showroom and didn't charge us for the improvements; he made a birthday party for me at the trade show and made sure that the best customers were sent our way. I was overwhelmed with emotion at the wonderful way in which he treated me.

Bruce had been a student at McGill University and he was involved in two sports. He was on the football team, the Redmen, at McGill and he was also on the wrestling team. He had trained at the Snowdon YMHA at the time when I was the coach of the Y wrestling team.

My attitude then, and my attitude now, was to give as much extra effort as possible and to be as nice as possible to my wrestling students – to everyone for that matter. As I learned from my father, and as I learned from Mr Rothschild, it is important to act in this way for the pure pleasure of giving. The way in which Bruce treated me was all the proof I needed that the Tanakh's invocation to "cast thy bread upon the waters for you shall find it after many days" is the best way to live.

* * *

When things work out, as they did with Bruce Miller and the American Home Furnishings Alliance, it is easy to see how my belief in helping others where possible and always giving, as my father put it, "a little more" works to everyone's benefit. Even though life is complicated and this philosophy doesn't always bring its intended results, my belief in it is unwavering.

There were times when I made a hiring decision that didn't work out. One of the executives I hired to manage our Toronto operation, for instance, violated Jaymar policy in a way that served to enrich him at the expense of our retail clients. His activities bordered on the criminal and of course the employee was fired.

From my perspective that was not the end of the story. I had no desire to change my personal policy of trying to help people where I could and rewarding those who deserved it. But I had to protect myself from those who would take advantage of me. I hit on a brilliant and simple solution to the problem.

In situations when I was about to make a significant decision about hiring, or if I had a question about the personalities behind a deal, I made certain that Eleanor had the opportunity to meet the person or people with whom I was about to enter into business. I would arrange a dinner or some similar event at which Eleanor could meet the person. Her judgment was better than mine and I valued her opinion. She was accurate in her assessment most of the time, and her choices usually worked out. Because I followed her advice I was able to surround myself with an excellent team of managers and suppliers – people with whom I am friendly to this day.

Our customers had faith in us. When a retailer couldn't make it to a trade show, for instance, he or she would call me and ask me to pick out two or three models that I thought were best suited to their market and send them to the store. Customers who made this request, a request they would not make of our competitors, were always pleased with the models and the price I chose for them, and never asked for return privileges. There were also times when a retailer would submit an order through one of our sales representatives and, much to the dismay of the salesman, I would call the client directly to say that his order was not in his business interest, because one or more of the products he ordered would not sell in his market. I recommended changes that benefited the customer but weren't always to Jaymar's short-term advantage. I was a long-term thinker and I wanted the customer to be happy; I sought a relationship with the client. In this way Jaymar would benefit from repeat business well into the future.

As the 1980s drew to a close business at Jaymar improved to the extent that I didn't have to worry about money. It was a pleasure for me to go to work each day because I enjoyed working with our people; and it was a pleasure to deal with our customers and our suppliers. For me, doing all of this was, in a word, fun. I derived a great deal of enjoyment during this period, as I had a feeling of security for the first time in my business life. I knew that Jaymar was on the right path and that it would enjoy continued success if we stuck to our management principles. It was a particular and meaningful pleasure for me to be able to put into practice the lessons I had learned from my father when I was a child of eleven or so in Szikszó.

In the early 1990s I instituted a profit-sharing program at Jaymar. I wanted to model it on other programs of a similar nature, but I couldn't find any, so I designed the plan on my own. Ten percent of the profits (a substantial amount!) were set aside to be divided among all the employees of the company. Only the unionized employees in the factory did not participate in the program because their union contract prohibited it. Otherwise, everyone else, from the receptionist who was the first contact for the people who visited our offices right up to senior management, participated in the program. The department heads were allotted a certain proportion of the profits to divide among their staff on the basis of their performance. The fact that the bonus was awarded on merit encouraged people to live up to my philosophy to always "make it better."

My management practices meant that Jaymar could always get the best work from the best people in a happy and productive environment.

* * *

Jaymar employed over three hundred people at its Terrebonne facility and took its role as the town's largest employer very seriously. I made it my business and the business of the company to participate in civic events. My personal relations with the mayor of Terrebonne were excellent right from the start, and I was gratified that he felt comfortable in coming to me when the city needed help with a special project. He approached me, for example, when the city wanted to build a sports arena and I was happy to lend my support to the plan. Jaymar contributed funds to the project and I assisted in the city's fundraising efforts.

I called on the other business owners in the region to get them to make financial contributions to the arena. Thanks to our combined efforts the city was able to build a great sports arena, used mostly by the youth of the region. This was the first facility of its kind in the city. Prior to its construction the kids had to play hockey exclusively on outdoor rinks – which was perhaps only a small inconvenience to them but a large problem for the parents who had to watch the games outdoors in the cold winters. The Complexes Sportifs Terrebonne is still in use today.

When the city wanted to build a theatre for live performances, Jaymar once again did its best to help. At no charge we manufactured the furniture that was necessary to outfit the theatre. Like the sports complex, the Théâtre du Vieux-Terrebonne is still in active use today and is the venue for many concerts and other live performances.

At the time of the celebration of Terrebonne's 325th anniversary, Jaymar was once again pleased to help. We were able to lend our support to the events that the city planned under the able leadership of the mayor, Jean-Marc Robitaille. I served on the organizing committee along with other businessmen and civic leaders. We worked hard to make sure the celebrations were successful and I was gratified to have had the chance to work on this committee.

\* \* \*

As a member of the board of directors of the Association des Fabricants de Meubles du Québec I had the opportunity to meet with representatives of both the provincial and federal governments. Both levels of governments provided grants to furniture manufacturers in order to help them innovate and be more competitive. They provided funds to support the purchase of new machinery and grants to subsidize the costs of exhibiting in the United States. Jaymar was grateful to benefit from these grants and subsidies.

In addition to its government relations work, the association also owned the national trade exhibition that took place in Toronto every year. Our association leased the building where the trade show was held. There were trade associations in most of the other provinces but the Quebec Association was the most important because of its control of the trade show in Toronto. Manufacturers from the rest of Canada had no option but to exhibit in the trade show we held and this gave our association a great deal of power in the industry. The Toronto trade show was a financial boon to the association, as it collected fees from the manufacturers who exhibited at the show on a one-off basis, and from companies, such as Jaymar, who had a permanent showroom in the building.

I was honoured when the board elected me president of the Association des Fabricants de Meubles du Québec in 1994. At the time that I was elected president, Quebec manufacturers dominated the furniture industry in Canada. The association had more than 125 members and there were in excess of fifty thousand people working in the furniture industry in Quebec. As president I had the opportunity to meet with business people from other industries as well as with my colleagues from furniture manufacturers from across Canada.

There were additional perks to being the president of the association, not the least of which was that Jaymar was able to occupy the best showroom in the building we leased in Toronto. But there were other less obvious benefits that gave me the opportunity to plan for the future of Jaymar. The information I had access to as president went to the membership soon after I learned it – it was an important part of the association's mandate to keep its members informed as to government policy – but I seemed to be able to make better use of it than many of my colleagues.

I was president of the Association des Fabricants de Meubles du Québec at the time that the Mulroney government in Ottawa was negotiating the Free Trade Agreement (FTA) with the United States. Thanks to the weakness of the Canadian dollar in relation to the American, Jaymar had been doing a good business in the United States for some time. I knew that the FTA, once signed, would allow us greater access to markets in the United States, and so I prepared to expand Jaymar's presence in the American market.

In addition to this, the president of the association had an automatic seat on the Conseil du patronat du Québec – the most important business organization in the province. The Conseil, as it was popularly known, advised the government on all its economic policies. Like the Association des Fabricants de Meubles du Québec the Conseil was involved with the negotiations for the Free Trade Agreement. I enjoyed working with the federal and provincial governments, although I was more than a little taken aback at the ways in which they spent taxpayers' money. Each of the meetings I attended – and I attended a lot of them – usually included an expensive lunch or dinner as part of our working day.

I applied the same standards to the association as I did to Jaymar – I found a way of doing things better. The first thing I did was to fire the executive director of the association. I found that he was spending too much money on things such as travel and entertainment that were of almost no benefit to the association members. I hired a replacement who was more in tune with my notion of how the association should be managed. The new executive director did excellent work and remained with the association for thirty years, until he retired.

In addition to this I engineered the purchase of a condominium for the association to use for its offices, on St Urbain Street south of René Lévesque Boulevard. Before I became president, it had been renting office space. I thought that it would be more beneficial to own the space we used, to enrich ourselves in a way, rather than enriching a landlord. In fact, the condo-office we purchased had more space than we needed, so we were able to rent the unused space, thereby providing us with enough income to cover *our* occupancy costs.

It gave me great pride to have been elected to the presidency of the association as it meant that my colleagues believed I had made an important contribution to our industry. I was very pleased that the work of the association, such as providing business information about the credit-worthiness of customers and providing access to government grants, helped its members grow their businesses.

\* \* \*

I was able to work on civic committees and the board of the Association des Fabricants des Meubles du Québec because I had a group of executives who were capable of running Jaymar during the times I was absent. Guy Patenaude, the Canadian Sales Manager, was my second in command. He was the man who replaced me when I was away.

Another of the core group of managers was Tony Troia. He was the Production Manager. He had solid experience and was well informed on all matters concerning the production and manufacture of furniture. He was more than capable of ensuring that our product line was of the highest quality.

After the company's profit-sharing program was established, I made certain to go a step further with Guy and Tony: I provided them with equity in the company. They paid for their shares out of money they received from the profit-sharing plan. I made Guy and Tony shareholders because they were excellent executives. As stakeholders in the company, they went well beyond the duties of their jobs and did everything they could, which included working long hours, to improve the profitability of Jaymar.

My motives in selling Guy and Tony equity in Jaymar were complex and varied. I wanted to reward them for their excellent work and provide a form of motivation that only owning equity can give. I also had a more personal reason. I knew that at some point in the future I would want to sell the company and retire. There was no one in my family who could take it over. I believed that if the key employees were also shareholders they would be able to manage the company for the new owners, whoever they turned out to be, and I would be free to leave. I had no desire to remain in my company as an employee. When the time came to sell Jaymar, my partners would, because of their equity holdings, gain financially from the sale of their shares.

Another step that I took was to hire Bruno Matthieu as the Office Manager and Controller. A little background here. Jaymar had employed an office manager and bookkeeper by the name of Morris Soifer. He and Auntie Annie had handled the bookkeeping, and he had looked after other administrative details as well. Morris was a capable bookkeeper but he was not a dynamic type of person. He never came up with any ideas. He did his job and that was it. He and Annie were loyal employees and I trusted both of them without hesitation. (Although I should add that Morris, unlike Auntie, was not the type of person who would call a supplier to explain that it had undercharged us. His attitude was that it was the supplier's tough luck and they should pay more attention to detail.)

Jaymar was one of the first companies in the furniture industry in Canada to adapt to the use of computers, and Morris was instrumental in helping me to automate the company. We purchased a second-hand computer system from Domtar. In those days, the days before PCs, computers were massive pieces of equipment. To get the main frame into the office we had to remove part of a window and bring it in by crane. The main frame was housed in a special room with a dedicated air conditioning and humidity control system, in order to ensure that it was neither too warm nor too dry. Morris also worked with the programmer to adapt the computer to our needs.

When Morris left the company in the mid-1990s, after working at Jaymar for over twenty years, I determined to replace him with an executive who would go beyond keeping the company's books and would be in a position to offer advice and assistance on all aspects of the business. I spread the word among my friends and contacts in Terrebonne that I was looking for someone with an accounting background. And that is how I met Bruno Matthieu. He was referred to me by François Duval, a notary with whom I was friendly. Bruno was a chartered accountant who lived in Terrebonne and worked for a firm of accountants who had offices in Montreal. He loved living in Terrebonne but didn't like the commute to Montreal. I found something very sympathetic about Bruno from our first meeting. I offered him a job and asked him what he was looking for by way of salary. He told me that he wanted $30,000. I told him that I would pay him $35,000 and for that money I expected him to be available to me whenever I needed him. If I wanted to call him on Sunday night to discuss a business problem, then I expected him to be available to discuss it. I thought about business all the time and I wanted my top people to do the same when necessary. I told him that in six months I would know for certain if he had the kind of business spirit that

I required and at that time one of two things would happen. Either I would decide that he was not the right man for the job and we would part company with no hard feelings or I would raise his salary to $40,000 because he had met my expectations.

The accounting firm that I used thought that my unconventional hiring practices and my insistence that it is best to pay a little more in order to get a lot more were crazy. But this was my preferred approach and it worked out well for Jaymar. Bruno exceeded my expectations and I discussed all sorts of matters relating to the administration of Jaymar and I found him to be, at all times, a good sensible man. His solid advice was influential in many of the decisions that I made throughout the 1990s.

Guy in sales, Tony in production, Bruno in accounting, and Monique in HR were the people I most relied on in the Canadian office when I had to make an important business decision. There was a fifth person on whom I depended very heavily – our US sales manager, Gary Zuckerman. He had worked in his family's furniture store before he came to work for Jaymar. This gave him a wonderful sense of what our retail customers needed from us in the way of sales support. In addition to his general knowledge of the furniture market, he was able to provide me with specific information on how to make a product that would sell well in the American market.

We learned that the US market was very different from the Canadian. The major difference is that Canadians are not, as a rule, as heavy as the Americans. Canadians are influenced by European designs and generally speaking they want harder, lower seating with less depth. In order to accommodate the fact that Americans are larger than Canadians and Europeans we had to make furniture that had deeper, softer seating. To put it another way: the Americans required a different "ass appeal" in their furniture than the Canadians. Gary was instrumental in helping me understand the importance of the differences in ass appeal between Americans and Canadians. Once we mastered and designed for these differences, our American sales increased dramatically.

I wanted to surround myself with a key group of executives for two basic reasons. The first and most obvious was that I wanted the best people to advise me when I had to make an important decision. I wanted people with whom I could discuss things in an efficient manner and, most importantly, people who had a very fast grasp of the problem and who could offer good advice without wasting time over discussing things. In this regard, Guy, Tony, Monique, Bruno, and Gary were excellent. Looking to the future, I had a second goal that I wanted to achieve with these people.

In 1999 at the furniture show in High Point, North Carolina, I was approached by a group of Chinese businessmen who wanted to get into the furniture business in Canada. They told me that if I gave them my designs they could manufacture them more cheaply than I could at my factory in Terrebonne. They went on to propose that I turn over my manufacturing to them and in return they would ensure that I had lower production costs and that I would have the exclusivity to the designs in the Canadian market. At our initial meeting they told me that I would also have the rights to sell their other models, on an exclusive basis, in the Canadian market. This appeared to be an interesting proposition for me as it would allow me to devote myself to design and sales, and I wouldn't have to worry about production, leaving me more time to spend with my family. The Chinese businessmen and I agreed to meet for breakfast the following morning to discuss the matter further.

In the short time between our first meeting and breakfast the next morning, the Chinese changed the terms of the deal they had offered. Now, less than twenty-four hours later, they told me that they could not give me the exclusive rights to the Canadian market but only those to the Quebec market. This "bait and switch" approach to business made me very suspicious of them. I had seen what had happened in the apparel trade. The Chinese took over the manufacture of American and Canadian products and killed off most of the manufacturers in those two countries. I knew that if I gave them my designs and allowed them to sell into the Canadian market they would soon put me out of business. There was already some evidence that the lower prices of Chinese-manufactured furniture were pushing Canadian furniture out of the market. This, in spite of the fact that the quality of the Chinese product was lower than the Canadian.

My breakfast meeting with the Chinese pushed me into making a decision that I had been considering for a while – a decision that related directly to my ensuring that I had a solid group of executives in the company.

As the twentieth century drew to a close I had come to the conclusion that it was time to sell Jaymar. I was sixty-seven years old and had been earning my own living for well over fifty of those years. I wanted to take things a little easier and devote myself to my children and grandchildren. I had prepared the groundwork by ensuring that whoever purchased Jaymar would have a talented team of executives to manage the company, allowing me a graceful exit.

Very soon after my meeting with the Chinese, while I was still at the trade show in High Point, I called Ralph Stump, an agent I knew. He was in the business of arranging the sale and merger of furniture companies. I told him I was ready to sell Jaymar and that I wanted him to handle the listing. We met and worked out a commission agreement. I showed him our financial statements and took pride in his comment that he had not seen a furniture company that was more profitable.

In the course of our first conversation I gave him the name of a venture capital firm that specialized in the acquisition of furniture companies, which had approached me – the Rivers Company from Tennessee. The Rivers Company owned a number of furniture manufacturers but none of them made leather-upholstered products. They wanted to add a company that specialized in this type of furniture. Jaymar was the industry leader in leather-upholstered furniture so it made sense that the Rivers Company wanted to acquire us. Their long-term plan was to take their companies public, and to do this they had to have a complete and diversified line of furniture manufacturers in their portfolio of companies.

At first Ralph wondered why I needed him, if this firm had already approached me. I told him I had never sold a company before and I wanted an expert to handle the deal. Ralph opened negotiations with the Rivers Company and brought in other potential buyers as well. The Rivers Company made an offer that I found acceptable, and they did their due diligence. They found, as I knew they would, that Jaymar was very well managed and that we had margins that were in excess of industry norms.

In fact, the Rivers Company couldn't believe that our gross profit was, on average, about double the norms for the furniture industry. The company had their accountants select certain products that we manufactured and they did a detailed cost analysis, down to the number of nails we used, of each item. They discovered that, for these pieces of furniture at least, the gross profit was even better than our company average. Once the Rivers Company had completed their examination of Jaymar, the deal closed. All in all, it was a fair and acceptable deal for both sides.

The financial terms were fair and acceptable but I have to admit that I had ambivalent feelings about selling the business I had worked so hard to create. I had poured my heart and soul into Jaymar and built a heritage business. I never forgot in whose honour I named the company, and that made it all the more difficult to walk away from it. But in the end I knew that selling the company was the right thing to do, so I signed on the dotted line.

As a result of their due diligence, the Rivers Company wanted me to join their corporation to help it organize the other companies it owned so as to make them as efficient and as profitable as Jaymar. I considered their offer for a while but in the end, after our deal had closed, I decided that I wanted less responsibility not more.

Only three months had elapsed from the time I called Ralph Stump to the closing of the sale with the Rivers Company. This meant that Jaymar was sold before Chinese manufacturers could become established in the American and Canadian markets. I knew that in the months following the sale of Jaymar in the year 2000, sales of Canadian manufactured furniture would go downhill very fast as a result of competition from the Chinese. However, because it had quality built into its products and its management, Jaymar didn't suffer to any great extent. It remained profitable.

The Rivers Company didn't keep Jaymar for very long. In 2003 it sold Jaymar to a company called Shermag, which had a portfolio of eleven furniture companies in Quebec. When the recession hit a few years later, in 2007, Shermag lost most of its holdings and filed for bankruptcy. However, Jaymar was still profitable, and the trustee in bankruptcy sold the company to one owned by the Darvou family.

In the beginning the Darvou family put Marcel Dufresne in charge of the company. Marcel was an engineer I had hired and he remained with the company following its sale to the Rivers Company and to Shermag. He had a first-rate knowledge of the furniture industry and his appointment ensured that Jaymar continued to be well run and profitable.

In 2009 Marcel left the company and the Darvou family made the wise decision of putting their sales manager, Daniel Walker, in charge. Daniel knew the business and was able to manage it successfully for the Darvou family. Finally, after managing the company for five years, Daniel made the Darvou family an offer to buy the company. They accepted, and the deal closed in 2014.

Following his purchase of the company, Daniel got in touch with me and invited me to visit the factory. I was thrilled to accept his invitation, as I was always happy to kiss the girls and hug the guys who had been so much a part of my life. I offered to provide any help I could. I told Daniel that I didn't want any money for this; my main interest, my only interest, was that the company do well so that my former employees, the people whose hard work I so appreciated, would continue to have jobs.

Daniel Walker summed up my feelings about the company when he said, "I didn't buy a furniture company; I bought Jaymar."

# 9

# Looking Forward, Looking Back

The emotional impact of selling Jaymar took a while to really hit me. On the first day following the sale of the company I woke up and got ready for work in the same way that I had every other day for the previous forty-four years. Eleanor must have thought I had lost my mind. "Where are you going?" she asked. "You don't own the business anymore."

Leaving a business that I had poured my heart and soul into for most of my adult life was not as simple as handing over the factory keys to the new owners. It had taken me many, many years to make Jaymar an industry leader. In the years preceding the sale, when Jaymar was at its apogee, I truly enjoyed the fruits of my labours. I knew that the company's success was a team effort and was due to the hard work of all its employees, whether the executives who worked in the office or the guys who swept the factory floor.

I was emotionally attached to the people I worked with and I knew I would miss them. I was just as attached to the customers and suppliers with whom I had built relationships over the years. My relationships with the people I worked with went well beyond the nuts and bolts of business; we liked each other and enjoyed interacting with one another on a personal level.

Finally, and from an emotional perspective, most importantly, at Jaymar I always had the sense that I was needed; running the company gave me a sense of fulfilment. The business was a part of me twenty-four hours a day. Even today, when I walk on Mount Royal with Eleanor and she points out the fall colours of a tree, when I look at it I don't see a tree, I calculate how many sofas we could make from the tree.

Leaving the people that I worked with for such a long time is a little like having someone close to you dying after a close relationship of forty-four years. I looked forward to living without the stresses involved with running a business but I knew I would miss the daily activity, the sense of being fulfilled by my work, and especially the people who had been such a part of my life.

And so I began my retirement.

* * *

As I said in an earlier chapter, one of my favourite things to do when I was a kid growing up in Szikszó was to accompany my father to work. I enjoyed working in the grain-trading warehouse with him and I enjoyed working on the farm we had. My father and I spent as much time with our workers as possible. We were interested in their lives and wanted them to feel a part of our enterprise. My father wanted to know if the workers had concerns with the work he assigned them, and if he found that they did have problems he would make it his business to find solutions. For example, the grain that came into our warehouse arrived in very heavy sacks. It required two men to hoist a sack of grain onto a truck. From talking to his workers, my father realized that it would be better if there were a third set of hands (not to mention muscles and a strong back) to help get the sack off the ground. Father made sure that he was available to help with the heavy lifting to make the job a little easier and ensure that the workers didn't injure themselves.

I applied the same principles to my own business. I spent as much time as I could in the factory talking to the workers, sharing breaks and lunches with them, in order to be certain that their concerns were heard and their needs respected. It was the work force at Jaymar who came up with the ideas that served to improve our manufacturing process. I was able to put many of these ideas into practice and make sure we were making the best product possible. A good suggestion was always rewarded. My father's examples from all those years ago were very much a part of the corporate culture at Jaymar.

I had achieved a business success beyond my imagining when I first stepped onto Canadian soil in 1948 – and now I determined to reap the rewards of all that I had achieved and devote myself to the people and things that I loved. First and foremost among these were Eleanor and our daughters and grandchildren.

After Eleanor and I married we rented a small apartment on Dupuis Avenue. Many in the postwar middle-class were settling there, but it was not itself a very affluent neighbourhood. The apartment was conveniently located so that I could walk to the Snowdon YMHA when I wanted to train there. It was also not too far from Eleanor's parents' home on Clanranald Avenue.

When our oldest daughter, Marla, was born in 1958, I had only been in business for two years and wasn't able to draw a very big salary. I had borrowed $500 from the business to pay for our honeymoon and I had to pay that back. I paid $10 each week so it took me almost a full year to pay back what I owed. Eleanor couldn't work because she became pregnant a year or so after we got back from our post-wedding travels in Europe. I wasn't worried about the future; I had started out with nothing and I knew that I would make it in my new business. But I wanted the best for my wife and for our child.

I had a lot of contacts in the furniture business and I was able to buy the things we needed from my friends and colleagues at wholesale prices – or better. The only luxury we had was a Jaymar sofa! We couldn't afford a television set, even if one of my contacts had been willing to sell me one at a discount. I refused to buy things on time. I believed that it would be a very bad idea to start married and business life by taking on debt for things that were not absolute necessities. Eleanor and I saved our money and we were able to buy a TV about six months after we moved into our first apartment.

That apartment only had one room – a living room – and a kitchen and after Marla was born we all slept in the same room. Eleanor and I slept on the Jaymar Make-A-Bed sofa and, of course, Marla slept in her crib. After about two years of living in our cramped apartment on Dupuis we were able to afford a house in Chomedey, a bedroom suburb north of Montreal.

When our second daughter, Aviva, was born in April of 1961 the business was becoming more profitable and I was able to draw a larger income. But my main concern was not money. Eleanor and I were very worried about Aviva. She was premature and weighed only 2.5 kilos (about 5.5 pounds) at birth. Our baby had to stay in the hospital in an incubator and the tension of worry didn't leave me until Aviva came home and we realized that everything would be fine.

Once we were assured that Aviva was a healthy baby I again turned my attention to business. Things continued to improve at Jaymar and I found my place in the business community in Montreal. As my business grew so did my reputation and just as it had always been my policy to help others whenever I could, I found that other businessmen were willing to help me when I needed it. Business associates offered me everything from discounts on product to lists of customers. The business was growing – each year was more profitable than its predecessor.

I also continued to devote myself to wrestling. I had to be very organized in order to keep at the sport I loved and I trained on a daily basis. My day started at 7:30 in the morning when I left for work, and after a full day at the office I made my way to the gym at about 6:00 in the evening, to spend two and a half hours training. I entered and won competitions. One of the unanticipated benefits of being a successful athlete and businessman is that it gained me positive notoriety in the Jewish community. It pleased me that the Jewish community of Montreal took reflected glory in my success.

Weekends were for Eleanor and the children. And after the first couple of years of working ten-hour days I cut back so that I could spend time in the late afternoons with my daughters. I continued to devote my evenings to training at the YMHA. In other words I was busy from very early in the morning until night-time.

Eleanor and I and our two daughters had a very comfortable life, but I still hoped to have a son so we decided to have another baby. Our third daughter, Judith, was born in 1965. Even though I had wanted a son, I was thrilled with Judith. She was a very loveable child and grew into a wonderful person. Like me she is interested in physical fitness and as an adult became a fitness trainer.

In the end the sex of my children made no difference to me. The important thing was that I had a happy, healthy family and we had a great life together. Of course as soon as children grow up, they want to leave the family home and start life on their own. Marla was the first to leave home. She went to design school in Florida. The plan was that she would study design and return to Montreal to work with me at Jaymar.

Following her graduation and until she and her husband, Perry Birman, moved back to Florida, Marla worked at Jaymar. She helped design new furniture and was in charge of the showrooms. She used her skill to decorate Jaymar's three showrooms; one each in Montreal, Toronto, and High Point, North Carolina. Under Marla's direction the Jaymar showrooms were furnished and accessorized in the forefront of home fashion – beautifully decorated in a way that communicated comfort and style. In addition to doing all of this Marla established her own business as a decorator. When she moved to Florida she again set herself up in business as a home decorator and, in addition to all her volunteer work, made a success of it.

Aviva too came to work at Jaymar, after she finished high school at just about the time that Nick and I were dissolving our partnership. She started off in customer service and looked after shipping and transportation, including the organization of shipping our furniture to the United States. She learned all the aspects of the business and she loved it as much as I did. She started every morning by bringing me a coffee and a kiss. This made my day. When I sold the business, Aviva was very unhappy. She would have happily taken over the operation of the company if I had agreed to stay on. I had to explain to her that the reason I was selling the company was that I no longer wanted the pressure of running it. A less loving child than Aviva might have resented my decision but she understood my motives and supported them. By that time she was married to Harold Staviss and, instead of taking over Jaymar, she devoted her time to her family and other interests.

Judith also came to work at Jaymar in product development. She went to McGill University for a couple of years but didn't feel cut out for university life. After she left McGill she worked at Jaymar for a few years, until, like her older sister, she and her children moved to Boca Raton.

Eleanor and I cherish the time we spend with our grandchildren and, like all grandfathers, I could easily write another book filled with the things that my grandchildren have done that gave us pleasure. However, my oldest grandson, Brett, did something exceptional, something that very few grandchildren have done for their grandfathers, I'm sure.

In 1999, when he was twelve years old, he was preparing for his Bar Mitzvah. Brett knew that I hadn't had the opportunity to celebrate this rite as I was imprisoned in Auschwitz when I was twelve years old. Without telling his parents, he came to me and suggested that we have a joint Bar Mitzvah. I was honoured but I didn't want to intrude on his special day, and at first I refused. But he wouldn't take no for an answer so we found a compromise. In the end, I had my Bar Mitzvah on the Friday, so as to make certain that he was the centre of attention at his Bar Mitzvah, which was held on the following day, Saturday.

Celebrating my Bar Mitzvah at the ripe old age of sixty-seven started me thinking about my past. The happy memories of my childhood were at first overshadowed by the difficult years that followed. But the past, in one way or another, is never as far away as we think, and slowly but surely I began the process of confronting it. In 2004 Eleanor and I and our two oldest grandchildren took a trip to Szikszó and Auschwitz, and this started me on the path that ended with the writing of this book.

I have to admit that I was a little nervous about dredging up unpleasant memories. In the process of writing this book I endured many sleepless nights as I relived so many awful events. But overall, there have been more pleasant and joyous events in my life than unpleasant ones and it is the memories of the good times that I cherish. I cherish them without denying all those elements that made my life what it is.

\* \* \*

Retirement also gave Eleanor and me the freedom to travel, and we took lots of opportunities to attend operas in Italy and visit art galleries and museums all over the world. One of our trips took us to Germany, particularly to Berlin – an open city since the destruction of the wall. We decided to pay a visit to the Holocaust Memorial. We found the experience very moving; even after the passage of so many years I was overcome with emotion when reminded of my past. As we were leaving the museum we came across a group of secondary school students and their teacher. I am a naturally gregarious and communicative person and when I overheard the teacher talking to her students about the meaning of the museum I couldn't stop myself from joining the conversation.

"I was there," I stated in my basic German, a language I first learned in school and then in Auschwitz, and later practised on my business travels to Germany. At first the teacher and the students didn't quite grasp my meaning. I think they took me to be a doddering old man stating the obvious – that I had visited the memorial. But after a moment or two they understood that I meant that I had been in one of the camps. This opened a floodgate of interest from the students and their teacher. The teacher told the students that they were lucky to have the opportunity to meet a survivor of the camps. In a mixture of German and English (the teacher spoke English and some of the students also had a grasp of the language) I told them my story and responded to their questions. The students were in awe of the fact that they had had the chance to meet and talk to someone who had lived the history they were learning about.

For my part, I was gratified by their honest interest in the past. I was aware of the strong feelings of guilt that German children experienced regarding their country's past and its desire, so many years before they were born, to destroy European Jewry. My feeling is that if these young people learn from the mistakes of their forbears they will not repeat them. I was so moved by the open-mindedness of these students that I found it impossible to bear them any ill will. This experience somewhat mitigated the negative emotions I felt while visiting the memorial.

I had done a lot of travelling for business, and Eleanor and I spent as much time as we could in Florida visiting our two daughters and their families who lived there. I had purchased a house in Boca Raton in 1995, but my work prevented us from using it for

more than five or six weeks a year. Now that I had retired, we were
able to spend more time with our children and grandchildren in
Boca Raton. I am the kind of person who has to have a project to
work on and improve, and I used the opportunity of living in Boca
to improve my golf game.

* * *

It was not only difficult to leave Jaymar; it was also difficult for me
to leave the many friends I had made in the town of Terrebonne.
When I first came to the town in 1968 its population was around
five thousand, a town with only six policemen. When I left in 2000,
the population had grown to over 65,000 and it now has a population of over 110,000. I came from the small town of Szikszó and I
had many happy memories of my childhood there. Terrebonne in
the early days reminded me of the Szikszó of my youth. It had the
small-town warmth of friendliness, where neighbour helps neighbour. I was pleased to participate in community activities, whether
it was to help with a charitable organization or with the construction of the sports arena. I was also very proud to show the people
of Terrebonne that I was Jewish. They had had little or no contact
with Jewish people up to that point and I had no idea what they
thought of Jews as a group. When I attended meetings I mentioned
my Jewishness at every opportunity but sometimes I overdid it.

From time to time I would need legal advice that related specifically to Jaymar's relationship with the Town of Terrebonne. In
these situations, I would consult the town's top notary, and that is
how I met Notary François Duval and his dynamic wife, Estelle
Couillard. Estelle was involved in the events of the town and
served on many committees. She and I became great friends and I
would frequently attend town meetings where she was present,
often serving on the committee that had organized the meeting.
When I wanted to avoid a question that I was asked, I used to kid
with the group and say, "I don't know, I'm Jewish." At one of the
meetings, Madame Couillard got really upset with me and said,
"Mr Reinitz, we know who you are – you're Mr Reinitz. Never
mind the rest." I took her exasperation with me as a compliment
in that it mattered very much to her and the town who I was but

my religion mattered not at all – and I preferred it that way. I also took this to show that I had been successful in showing the people I dealt with something of what it was like to be a Jew. And I felt that I was warmly accepted by everyone.

I became emotionally attached to the people of Terrebonne and when I left I received many cards and letters wishing me well and telling me that I was taking a piece of their hearts with me. At an honorary breakfast the town organized to bid me farewell, I made it clear that I was leaving a piece of my heart in Terrebonne. In 2004 at another event, a dinner honouring those who had contributed to the building of the town, I was again honoured, this time as a builder of the region of Île des Moulins with a plaque on the town's *Mur des bâtisseurs.*

\* \* \*

My retirement was a mixed blessing. I enjoyed being free of the day-to-day pressures of running a business and I was pleased to have more time to spend with Eleanor and our family. At the same time, I missed the challenge of running a business and, having been a general for so many years, I was not fully comfortable being a foot soldier. I thought about going into another business as a silent partner or investor and considered becoming a mortgage lender. But Eleanor convinced me not to go into any business that I didn't fully understand so I didn't take on any of these business opportunities.

I was fortunate to have sold Jaymar when I did. After 2000 the economy took a turn for the worse, Chinese imports made competition tougher, and Canadian and Quebec furniture industries suffered sales decreases. In spite of all the problems that occurred in the furniture industry over the years since I sold, I am proud to say that Jaymar has not only survived but has done very well as a manufacturer of a quality product, one of the few Canadian furniture producers to still be in business. Jaymar celebrated its sixtieth anniversary in 2016. I am pleased to be in a position to be able to assist the new owner of the company whenever he calls on me for advice.

\* \* \*

I loved the sport of wrestling and never stopped being involved in the Quebec and Canadian wrestling community. The wresting centre that I endowed – the George and Eleanor Reinitz Wrestling Centre – became one of the finest gyms in Canada for training in the sport. But it was more than the success of the wrestling centre that gave me pleasure. I greatly enjoyed hearing about the achievements of the people I trained who went on to lead very successful lives. I get a vicarious sense of excitement when I see the hard work they put into their training in order to compete successfully at the highest levels of the sport.

When we lived in Chomedey, I opened a training gym on the second floor of a shopping mall. I used the facility to offer training to the young people of the area. One of the kids I trained was a young boy by the name of Howard Stupp. He had a lot of talent and I encouraged him to continue in wrestling when he outgrew my Chomedey training centre. I became a coach and a mentor to him.

Howard continued to train and became a member of the McGill University wrestling team while a student there. He obtained a degree in engineering. I took a special delight in this, because it reminded me of the time when, as a newcomer to Canada, I was drafted onto the McGill wrestling team and told that if asked what I was studying, I should reply, "Engineering." Unlike me, Howard was a real engineering student. Following his engineering degree, he went on to get a law degree.

He continued in the sport and became an internationally recognized wrestler. Both the Canadian and Quebec governments supported him so that he could continue to train and compete. He competed in the Olympic Games in Montreal in 1976. Unfortunately, not long before competing in the Olympics, Howard had an appendix operation and wasn't up to his full capacity as a wrestler for the games. This handicap was not helped by the fact that his opponent in his first match was the person who went on to become the Olympic champion at those games. Howard made the Canadian Olympic wrestling team to compete in the Olympic games in Moscow in 1980, but because Canada boycotted those games he was unable to participate.

Following his graduation from law school, Howard got a job working with Stikeman Elliott, the law firm where Dick Pound was a partner. Dick was an ex-Olympian and a member of the governing board of the International Olympics Committee (IOC). He later became founder and president of the World Anti-Doping Agency. Dick thought that Howard would be an excellent addition to the legal department of the IOC. As a result, Howard joined the IOC based in Lausanne, Switzerland, and he soon became the head of the IOC legal department. Over the years we kept in touch, as was the case with many of the people I had trained.

Howard very kindly invited me to be a guest of the IOC at the Olympic games in Beijing in 2008, and he provided me with access to a car and driver, and privileges at all the VIP facilities, along with access to all the events that I wished to attend, including the opening and closing ceremonies. Wherever I went during the Olympics, I was with a group of dignitaries. We were served in separate dining rooms and offered special seating at the events. Howard went out of his way to ensure that I was treated with great respect during my stay in Beijing.

Following the Olympics Eleanor joined me in China and we had a wonderful vacation. I doubt that we would have had the opportunity to visit China had it not been for Howard's thoughtful generosity.

I remain in touch with Howard to this day. In fact, I do my best to keep in contact with as many of the people as possible from my days as a competitive wrestler and coach. I am pleased that my former students have benefited from participating in that great sport, and I am deeply touched by the many ways, large and small, in which they express their appreciation to me.

* * *

The past is always with us. It is important to honour it and remember it. But it is just as important not to let it ruin our present. I believe that it is critical to have a sense of humour about the events, no matter how terrible, of our lives.

I have done my best to stay in touch with other survivors of the Holocaust, even though, as time passes, our numbers are diminishing. Whenever I am with a group of other survivors, no matter what we are talking about, whether it be politics or business or our families, the conversation always returns to our days in the camps. I find that the best way to deal with the horror of those memories is to find a way to make a joke, a possibility that only exists because so much time as passed since those terrible years, and because I live in Canada. The jokes don't erase the memories; nor are they intended to. But they help to make the memories a little less painful.

I was fortunate to have learned from my father and from Mr Rothschild all those years ago in Szikszó that it is a privilege and a source of great satisfaction to be able to help others. I followed their example without the expectation of receiving anything in return. Mr Rothschild told me that even if someone throws a stone at you, you should throw back a piece of bread. It took me a long time to make this lesson a part of my life but I have to say that living by this rule gives me great satisfaction.

As a boy in school I learned to stand up to bullies and to protect the weak. It came naturally to me to make friends wherever and whenever possible. I don't think I would have survived Auschwitz, much less had the success I did in life, without the help of friends. In Auschwitz we shared any extra food we were able to acquire. If one of my friends managed to get an extra piece of bread, he would share it. Our expression, when dividing the extra food was, "you cut, I choose." I wouldn't have ended up in the furniture business if I hadn't wanted to find a way to bring my friend Karcsi to Canada. And I never would have made it to Canada without the help and influence of Mr Rothschild.

At this time of my life I have to count the blessings of my good fortunes. Eleanor and I are happy and able to enjoy our family, and it is wonderful to see that the younger generation have an attitude toward life similar to mine.

Some of my work ethic comes from my experience in wrestling where I learned to put out my best effort and always to be fair. I never tried to hurt any of my opponents. In any case, I didn't have to do that to come out on top. I also learned that sometimes we have to lose in life; it only makes us better and encourages us to try harder in the future.

At this time I know that I am in the twilight zone of my journey. I have done my best to remember all those who touched my life. There were times when the memories I recalled were very painful and caused me sleepless nights. But the happy times far outweighed the sad ones, and I am pleased to be able to honour at least some of the people who made my life what it has been and is. To mention every single good person who helped me throughout my life would take another book. But thinking back, I can't think of many people that I wish I had never met. And I don't hate anyone. I know that I could sometimes be demanding but I demanded as much, or more, of myself as I did from others.

\* \* \*

My reward is the pleasure of enjoying every one of my children and grandchildren and our great-grandchildren and I still also get satisfaction from interacting with the kids at the Reinitz Wrestling Centre. In my work there, I know I am influencing young people to be good citizens. This keeps me busy and at the end of the day – happy.

Experience taught me to be open to new ideas and methods of doing things. All of these elements came together to make me the person I am today. I've been very successful in life, I have a wonderful wife and a loving family, and this is the source of my pride and happiness. Finally and most important, I'm proud to be the heir to all that I learned and the love I received from my father and mother, even though it was only for a short time, all those years ago in Szikszó.

# Afterword

January 27 is my rebirth date. It was the day in 1945 when I again became George Reinitz and stopped being A 10,440. It was the day that the Soviet Army liberated me and my fellow *häftlings* from the Nazis.

I celebrate my rebirth day with a sense of sadness and anger, remembering all that I lost in the eight or so months that led up to it. I didn't know on that day that I was alone in the world, having lost my beloved family. As a youngster and as a young man I missed the warmth, comfort, and love of my family and regretted the fact that I no longer had my father's guidance. I've learned over the years to deal with this sadness and anger. These feelings will always be a part of my make-up, but it has been a very long time since they dominated my emotional life.

During my early years in Canada I struggled to come to terms with the anger I felt in response to all that I had been through. Hungary, the country I left behind, prized cultural and religious uniformity in the period when I lived there. It enforced this notion first by ostracizing those, primarily Jews and Roma, that it considered to be "others" – not Hungarians pure and true. And then Hungary sought our annihilation.

When I arrived in Canada in 1948 I discovered the possibility that a number of cultures could co-exist with one another. I learned that when problems and conflicts arose among the various groups that made up the population of Montreal they were settled without resorting to armed combat. And in the rare cases where conflicts ended in violence the majorities on both sides of the issue were quick to oppose it and de-escalate the situation.

I felt very much accepted in my new home and love it for all of that. After everything I had been through over time I developed a sense of peace and belonging. Today, I can't imagine living anywhere other than in Montreal. And when I am away I begin to feel restless; a feeling that dissipates only when I return to the city I call home.

Eleanor tells me that I shouldn't dwell in the past but focus on my good fortune, on all that I have. She is right. I have a lot to be thankful for. I have three beautiful daughters, seven grandchildren, two great-grandchildren, and two wonderful sons-in-law. I arrived alone in Canada in 1948 and now when we get together as a family there are eighteen of us. I worked hard and became a success in my adopted country and I am pleased and thankful for the opportunities that Canada has given me. In the taxes I pay each year, I take pride in being able to give something back to the country that has done so much for me. I am equally proud of the Reinitz Wrestling Centre, which Eleanor and I built as a training centre for Canadians, and indeed for wrestlers from around the world, to train with our great coaches under the supervision of Viktor Zilberman.

I am well aware that I paid a very high price for my good fortune. And I never forgot this. Young people, especially those who grew up in affluence in Canada and the United States, lead very sheltered lives. One of my reasons for writing this book is so that the youth of today and future generations will be aware that the good lives they enjoy have come at a price and that we must never forget this fact.

I also worry about the future. I see the tide of anti-Semitism rising again. In some cases it is concealed under the mantle of political correctness, but this is a very thin disguise for an extremely evil ideology. I see that once again European Jews do not feel comfortable in their home countries and that they are fleeing France and other nations. Luckily, now Israel is there to welcome them. I love and support Israel in every way I can, but still I want Jews to feel comfortable wherever they choose to live. I learned the hard way that if Jews don't stand up for themselves then no one will do it for them.

I know that my friends and family who grew up in the relative security of Canada and the United States have a different view. Their life experiences have taught them that it is best to talk things over, to negotiate and to find compromises so that we all get something of what we want. My life experiences have taught me a very different lesson; for me it is difficult to see the possibility of peace and compromise with people who want to annihilate you. There are times when compromise and negotiation are not possible. I hope that I am worrying for nothing and that those with different life experiences are right. But I see in the new anti-Semitism much of what I saw living in Europe in the 1930s and 1940s, and it worries me.

I never stopped being curious about the events of the past that so influenced my life and cost me my family. I learned, in bits and pieces, that the politicians and governments that could have and should have acted to save European Jews either did nothing or, worse, allied themselves with the Nazi Government by way of appeasement. In 1939 the MS *St Louis*, a ship carrying over nine hundred Jewish refugees from Germany, was turned away by both Canada and the United States. Roosevelt snuck out of the White House like a coward rather than meet with a delegation of rabbis in 1943. And the anti-Semitic policies of the Canadian government during that period are well known.

American businesses from IBM to Coca Cola did what they could to protect their economic interests in Germany. Henry Ford Sr, the auto-maker, was awarded and accepted the Grand Cross of the German Eagle Award from the Nazi Government in 1938. This was already five years after Dachau, the first concentration camp, was opened and three years following the promulgation of the Nuremburg Laws. Joseph Kennedy, the American ambassador to Great Britain, was an anti-Semite and an isolationist. He famously advised President Roosevelt to adopt a policy of isolationism with regard to the coming war in Europe. I've often wondered how many lives, Jewish and others, this advice and policy cost. In other words, at a time when the world knew or should have known about Nazi plans to rid Europe of Jews, those in power did nothing to help us.

As a young man, newly arrived in Canada, it took many years for my anger to subside. It became secondary to adjusting to my new life, getting married, starting and building my business, wrestling, and raising my family. The anger and frustration never left me and the more I learned of past events the worse these feelings became.

All of this was brought home to me recently when I read an article by Alan Dershowitz,* a prominent scholar and professor emeritus of law at Harvard University. In the article he talks about his feelings of anger and horror on a visit to the Auschwitz and Birkenau death camps where members of his extended family had been tortured and murdered. He goes on to describe the situation in Hungary when Jews were murdered and deported at a time when the Nazis were already in retreat. His description revived in me my feelings of anger and frustration as I recalled hearing about the blood of Rothschild Bácsi's daughters that seeped into the Danube, and the fate of my family as we were pushed into boxcars in a way that you would not treat animals, and shipped like garbage to imprisonment and death. My memory of my feelings of jealousy of the birds who could fly away while I was enslaved in Auschwitz came flooding back, this time not as envy but as fury.

There are still times when my anger so overwhelms me that I want to shout it out at whoever crosses my path. I have no wish for these feelings of outrage and enmity to abate. I want them to remain strong in me as an eternal flame to keep alive the memories of all those who suffered and died. And I especially want my children, grandchildren, and great-grandchildren to be aware of them so that they will be vigilant against the repetition of this history. As pleased as I am with all that I have accomplished in life, I never want to forget that politicians whom we so revere – Mackenzie King in Canada and Franklin Delano Roosevelt in the United States – did nothing to help the Jews of Europe, much less to save them. These men could have had the railway lines and bridges that carried us to the death camps bombed, yet they falsely claimed that this was not possible. Winston Churchill had the RAF bomb the railway lines in Hungary in July 1944 and when he five times requested that the Americans use their superior air power to bomb additional railway lines leading to the camps, the American undersecretary for war, John J. McCloy, refused to allow it.†

---

\* Alan Dershowitz, "A Visit to the Old and New Hells of Europe Provides a Reminder of Israel's Importance," Gatestone Institute: 17 May 2016.

† Martin Gilbert, CBE, "Churchill and the Holocaust: The Possible and Impossible," International Churchill Society 25th Anniversary Conference, US Holocaust Memorial Museum, Washington, 8 November 1993.

It is gratifying to know that Churchill spoke in favour of Jews and the Jewish state – he met in 1939 with Dr Chaim Weizmann, then president of the Zionist Organization and later the first president of Israel, and promised his support for a Jewish homeland after the war – and did what he could to help, often in conflict with his own political party.* Churchill's actions show what the leaders of Canada and the United States could have done if they had had the courage and the political will to do the right things. But they failed to follow Churchill's example and in so doing failed millions of innocent people, my family among them, who paid with their lives.

I hope that before I die, someone can explain to me the reason that we Jews are still hated rather than being honoured for our contributions to art, medicine, music, science, and countless other fields. Roosevelt and King, Kennedy and Ford are all dead now and treated as heroes. To me, there was nothing heroic about their behaviour and I find it tragic that they were never brought to justice – either in a court of law or in the court of public opinion.

Part of my motivation in writing my biography is to ensure that these men not be spared the judgment of history.

The other factor that motivated me to record my experiences is that I believe hatred has no place in our world. It serves only to divide us and deny opportunity to the vast majority of the people of the world who desire nothing more than peace and a safe and secure place to live.

\* \* \*

I have many things to be thankful for, many things I would not have had without Eleanor at my side. And so it is to her and to our children, grandchildren, and great-grandchildren that I lovingly dedicate this book.

* Ibid.

# Richard King's Acknowledgments

First and foremost I want to thank George Reinitz for giving me the privilege of working on his autobiography with him. The reader now knows what I learned over the last two or so years that George and I have been writing his book. George is truly an amazing person. He arrived in Canada in 1948 as a penniless sixteen-year-old after surviving the horrors of Auschwitz and less than ten years later he was the flag bearer of the Canadian team of athletes at the Maccabiah Games in Israel. He raised a family, built a business, became an accomplished athlete and a philanthropist. Like all those who know George, I am deeply touched by his warmth, his kindness, and his generosity of spirit.

I would like to thank Philip Cercone, Mark Abley, and the wonderful team at McGill-Queen's University Press. They provided intelligent guidance as George and I brought this book to completion. I also want to thank Jane McWhinney for the miracles of editorial work she performed on the manuscript, encouraging me, as George would put it, "to make it better."